Who Said Women Can't Teach?

Who Said Women Can't Teach?

Charles Trombley

Bridge Publishing, Inc.
South Plainfield, NJ

Publishers of:
Logos • Haven • Open Scroll

All Scripture quotations are from the
New American Standard Bible unless otherwise identified.
Used by permission.

Who Said Women Can't Teach?
© 1985 Bridge Publishing Inc.
All rights reserved.
Printed in the United States of America
ISBN 0-88270-584-9
Library of Congress catalog number: 85-072150
Bridge Publishing, Inc.
2500 Hamilton Blvd.
South Plainfield, NJ 07080

Dedication

This book is lovingly dedicated to Gladys, my wife and very best friend, for her encouragement, reading and criticism over two years of research and writing. Special thanks to Dr. John Rea, O.T. Professor at CBN University, for his scholarship in checking facts and language sources. Also to Dr. Judson Cornwall who set aside writing a book on the same subject and encouraged mine. And to the librarian at Oral Roberts University and for the use of the ORU library and reference sources.

Contents

Foreword

I have repeatedly been urged to write a book about women in the ministry, for my sister served with me in pastoring for nearly a dozen years, and my present pastor is a woman. I was already deep in research on such a book when I discovered that Charles Trombley was already involved in the same project. I volunteered to set my project aside until I had examined his manuscript. Now that I have carefully studied it I can see no reason for writing a book on this subject—Charles Trombley has covered the subject thoroughly and quite scholarly.

I believe that the truths expounded in this book can release many more of God's servants to the ministries God has implanted in them, and it should settle the spirits of many pastors who have needless doubts over the validity of women's ministries.

I highly commend this book to the Body of Christ.

Judson Cornwall
Philippians 4:4

1

Should Women Be Silent
in the Church?

The "woman" question isn't a simple issue. Instead, it is one of the most complex, emotional problems facing the Church. In March 1976, *Logos Journal* published an article about the Episcopalian debate, "Should Women Be Priests?" In 1983, *Christianity Today* devoted the best part of a whole issue to "Women At The Helm," paralleling the pros and cons of the ordination of women and the headship of men. Both sides of the issue were carefully represented but neither side solved the problem. Is it scriptural for women to minister, and if not, why not? Who forbids them? Tradition, cultural and sexual bias, or masculine pride?

Recently *The Charlotte Observer* printed a letter to the editor claiming that the only place for Christian women is in the home. Motherhood is their God-given role in life. A woman's role is to help her husband, the letter argued. Meanwhile, the Catholic Church continues to be swept by waves of dissent over the question of women clergy. One prominent Baptist leader rejects the Pentecostal experience because Pentecostals allow women to speak in church. The United Presbyterian Church's governing body requires that men and women be equally represented at all synods. Even the Bible is under attack: the National Council of Churches wants the Scriptures desexed by deleting all references to the masculinity of God, the male Lordship of Christ, or the headship of men.

Theologically, the camps are confused. One group lets women teach Sunday school if men are not present. Some denominations ordain women as full-time missionaries, and let them teach liberal arts subjects in their Bible colleges, sing in the choir, and pay tithes. But teaching from the pulpit? Never! The same women who function as teaching missionaries are denied that opportunity at home. Their sermonettes are acceptable only when the male pastor gives the benediction.

Other groups throw all caution to the wind. "Whosoever is called of the Lord may preach," they say, disregarding any Scriptures that seemingly contradict their attitude.

One fact is obvious: many are not sure just what the Scriptures really say about the role of women in ministry. In an interview with *Logos Journal* (March/April 1976) the Reverend William Folwell, Episcopal Bishop of Central Florida, stated, "But you know, Paul also said women weren't even supposed to speak in church, and we haven't paid attention to that for a long time!"

No one denies that there are unanswered questions. I recently taught on this exciting subject at a week-long conference at Duquesne University. After the sessions were over, several clergymen asked that I make sure they receive a copy of this study as soon as it is published. Intimately and frankly they confessed their doubts about what is and what should be.

The basic problem stems from one short passage attributed to Paul in 1 Corinthians 14:34-35:

Let the women keep silent in the churches; for they are not permitted to speak, but let them subject themselves, just as the Law also says. And if they desire to learn anything, let them ask their own husbands at home; for it is improper for a woman to speak in church.

There it is, just as the Word records it. It seems clear enough, but it raises several obvious questions that must be considered:

1. Who said women must be silent?
2. Why can't they speak and why is it shameful?
3. Must they be silent only in church, and if so, why?
4. Should they be silent at all times or only on special occasions?
5. Does this include praying, singing, praising and prophesying?
6. Is this restriction binding upon all women for all time or was it a local thing?
7. *Where and what is the law that underscores this restriction?*

Of course, there are other interesting questions such as:

"Why ask their husbands at home and what if the husband is a practicing pagan?"

"What does subjection have to do with silence?"

"Did Paul assume all women to be married?"

These are simple, logical and sensitive questions that must be answered if we're going to formulate an intelligent, scriptural answer.

The Traditional Interpretation and Its Problems

Let's assume this passage can be understood and accepted without any commentary. All women must remain silent during public worship since the Greek verb *sigao* means to be quiet, to hold one's peace.[1] What are the implications?

Theoretically women can't serve as missionaries since they would undoubtedly teach adults, including men, the way of salvation. They can't teach Sunday school. They can't sing in the sanctuary choirs: church music carries a message.

Many of the same churches who prohibit women teaching because of Paul's statement in 1 Timothy 2:12, "I do not allow a woman to teach," don't hesitate a second when inviting women to sing in the choir or as soloists. Frankly, I find it difficult, in light of the Scriptures, to separate this effective ministry from preaching, since only the method of delivery differs. The content of the message may be the same. Ephesians 5:18-20 clearly teaches that all Christians are to be speaking to one another "in psalms and hymns and spiritual songs, singing and making melody in your heart to the Lord"(KJV). Compare this statement with Paul's advice to the church at Colossae where they were to teach one another with the same songs, psalms and hymns (Col. 3:16). What Paul said is that psalms, hymns and spiritual songs are vehicles for teaching. Can one say that vocalists don't minister? Singers communicate biblical truths through the medium of music just as preachers communicate these same truths through the medium of talking. In either case, the human voice is used. One speaks, the other sings. Is one ministry more valid than the other?

Tradition demands that we neglect hundreds of Scriptures exhorting believers to raise their voices and praise the Lord in the midst of the congregation (e.g., Ps. 95). Praise is always vocal and at times exuberant and loud (Rev. 19:1-6). If by "silence" Paul meant "absolute silence," then all women must cease all praise.

I realize how outrageous this conclusion is, but we can't have it both ways, can we? Truth is consistent! Many commentators recognize this difficult problem. One priest explained it this way: "Paul meant the women can't preach publicly when adult

4

men are present. They can speak since Paul said they may pray and prophesy; they are only restricted from forgiving sins and ministering the Eucharist." Another explained: "He specifically addressed the unlearned women and told them to be quiet during the service. If they wanted information ask their husbands at home."

Recently a pastor told me it was "whispering" that was meant since Paul used the verb *lalein*. "It is not permitted unto them to *speak"(lalein)* in the church. But the same word is used in verse 39, "and forbid not to speak [*lalein*] in tongues." One Charismatic pastor said, "The only thing Paul forbade was teaching foundational truths. They can teach minor truths but the 'heavy stuff' belongs to the five-fold ministry." Susan Foh, author of *Women and the Word of God,* believes Paul referred to the traditional form of teaching involving questions and answers. "Woman would not be allowed to participate in it, for to do so would be to teach."[2] Perhaps the weakest explanation is the traditional one: The women sat on one side opposite the men and during the service they asked their husbands questions and it was this noisy spectacle that Paul quieted. However, there isn't any historical or scriptural evidence for this explanation.

Finally, there's the assumption of the liberal critics that although the Corinthian letter is indisputably Pauline, this passage was not part of Paul's original letter, probably added by an early scribe paraphrasing 1 Timothy 2:11-12 and added to this epistle as though Paul had actually written it. This argument undermines the trust Bible believers have in the divine inspiration and preservation of the Scriptures.

There is, however, some basis for the statement that Jewish women were separated from the men, both in the Temple and synagogues, but they did not sit opposite one another within talking distance. Under the Jewish system there was total separation of the sexes.

Separation was the principle upon which Temple worship was founded; it emphasized the distinction between God and man, Jew and gentile, men and women, priests and people. These various separations were symbolized by the different courts in the temple.[3] Although Herod's temple was completely segregated, the evidence indicates that segregation was a later development. Neither Solomon's temple, built in the tenth century B.C.E., nor Zerubabbel's temple, built in the sixth century B.C.E., had these separate courts. Just when the practice began is open to question, but we do know Herod's temple was totally segregated. According to the *Mishnah,* part of the Jewish Talmud, the Court of Women was surrounded by a gallery so that the women could observe from above without mingling with the men below.[4] The historian Josephus wrote that the women's court was fifteen steps above the men's court and entered by outside gates and stairways, completely isolating the women from the men.[5] These practices were based on the rabbis' understanding of Zechariah 12:12, which mentions the country mourning, the family separated, and the women apart.

Therefore, if silencing women in Christian assemblies is based upon a Jewish custom, it stands on flimsy interpretation by the rabbis and not on the Scriptures. Women didn't question their husbands during Jewish worhsip. They didn't say anything! The *Tosephta,* a rabbinical commentary, says, "A woman is not to come forward to read [from the Torah, the law]." The *Encyclopaedia Judaica* article on women states, "There was general agreement that a woman was not obligated to study Torah. As a result few women were learned." At the beginning of the Common Era, Jewish women weren't active participants in the synagogue or Temple services; they were spectators and listeners. Rabbi Eliezer said, "Whoever teaches his daughter the Torah is like one who teaches her obscenity."[6]

From the beginning of Israel's secular and religious history, the heart of Judaism has been the study and practice of the

Torah, the law of Moses. It governs every facet of Jewish daily life. By excusing women from studying and practicing the law, the rabbis maintained a sharp distinction between men and women and firmly established the second-class status of women in Israel. Rabbi Eliezer also said, "Rather should the words of the Torah be burned than entrusted to a woman."[7]

In fact, not only were the women separated and silenced in the synagogue and Temple, they were separated and silenced in their own homes as well, not eating meals with their husbands when guests were present. Some rabbis carried this subjugation even further: "One must not be served by a woman."[8] Unfortunately, this custom still exists in parts of the Middle East today. Women prepare the food and bring it to the door of the dining area where the youngest male brings it to the men and guests.

Therefore, the explanation that the Corinthian church was segregated along the lines of the Jewish system of worship is inaccurate. Jewish women weren't allowed to speak, learn, worship or discuss the law. They were completely *silent!*

Who Would Teach Them?

Would Paul, who revealed that the church fulfilled the prophecies regarding Israel, have patterned the Lord's New Covenant church after an outdated system? If Christ was the end of the law and its requirements, as Paul wrote in Galatians 3:19, how could the Church still be governed by the law?

It should be noted that 1 Corinthians 14:34-35 silences only those women with husbands, thereby excusing the unmarried, the divorced and widows: ". . . let them ask their own husbands at home." If this injunction was meant for all women, why did Paul single out the wives? Did he demand or expect all women to marry? If so, why did he strongly recommend (1 Cor. 7:7, 8) that the unmarried and widows remain as he was, unmarried? Or were the wives the only ones talking during the service? If so, are unmarried women allowed to speak publicly? Although these questions are difficult, they are legitimate, and they point out the overly simplistic explanations that have become commonplace. Further, we've assumed that this passage was Paul's own statement, directly contradicting his earlier instructions in 1 Corinthians 11:5 where he said women may publicly pray and prophesy. Logically, then, was this "silencing directive" his or was he quoting someone else? Is this passage a revelation from the Lord, or was Paul referring to something else?

Why Did Paul Write to the Corinthians?

All Bible scholars are acquainted with and should use what is called the HGC method of study. They must consider *H*istorical information, including the time, place, and cultural conditions surrounding the writing, the *G*rammatical structure of the passage in the original language, and the *C*ontextual evaluation of the passage, comparing it with other Scripture and writings to understand how particular words and phrases are used and translated elsewhere. This method isn't a cut-and-dried system, but it is helpful. Without these basic guidelines, some passages can be made to mean almost anything.

Many scholars have given "quickie" answers to 1 Corinthians 14:34-35 and 1 Timothy 2:12 and then closed the issue. The confusion which follows is primarily the result of not following their reasoning through to its logical conclusion. This is what John Calvin, the Reformer, did when commenting on these passages. He taught that women were created inferior and must be ruled by men. Therefore, he reasoned, men were created to control and rule women. As a Christian he was free to reason as he desired but his conclusions don't have to be accepted as truth.

Apparently, many teachers have missed the truth by not considering the cultural background of Paul's readers. Most of his epistles dealt with local problems, doctrinal errors peculiar to them, and questions that had been asked him. We must make allowances for these factors.

Why did Paul write his Corinthian letter? The church was in a state of division and disorder (1 Cor. 1:11-17), with Gnostics and Judaizers causing most of the trouble. Because Paul had "fathered" the church and worked with them for many months, they asked him for his advice and sent their questions in a letter (7:1). In his reply he addressed each of their questions separately with the phrase "now concerning" (7:1, 25; 8:1; 12:1; 16:1), and somewhere in his answer he alluded to their question. For example: "Now concerning things sacrificed to idols" is the way he took up this question; he then gave the answer. In chapter 9 he defended his apostleship against those who questioned his authority. Chapter 11 deals with the problem of men wearing head coverings like the women during public worship. Then in chapter 12 he took up another question by saying, "Now concerning spiritual gifts . . ." and for the next three chapters gave an in-depth teaching on the *charismata.* The controversial statement we're studying is part of this section. His Corinthian letter was written in response to several questions the church had asked him and each answer is preceded by "Now concerning."

In reference to the cultural aspect of women teaching, we might ask this question: "Why has the leadership role been traditionally male territory?" The answers are interesting if not entirely scriptural. Some argue that since God is male, His leaders on earth should be male. But this is faulty reasoning since God is neither male nor female but Spirit (John 4:24; cf. Mark 12:25). Others have explained by saying that since the Old Testament priests were men, the New Testament ministers must also be men. Finally, there's the argument based on the order of creation. Since man was created first, he was the leader. When the woman was later created she obeyed him.

9

The Real Problem in Corinth

The Epistles and the Acts of the Apostles record a recurring issue among the infant churches. Judaizers followed Paul everywhere he went, demanding that male converts be circumcised and observe the law of Moses in order to be saved (Acts 15:1-2). These Judaizers were Jews who believed Jesus was Israel's Messiah but refused to abandon their former traditions and customs even though the requirements of the law were fulfilled in Jesus Christ. Another factor in their persistent demands that the gentile believers observe their customs was that the new Christian community was accepted as another sect in Judaism along with the Pharisees, Sadduccees, and Essenes. Their thinking was, "Other converts to Judaism are circumcised and keep the customs of Moses, so why not these?"

However, Paul revealed that Christ was the end of the law for those who believe. The Mosaic customs and traditions were canceled by Christ's resurrection and the ushering in of the New Covenant. The Jewish reaction was inevitable. At times their resistance was violent and Christians suffered terrible persecution and abuse. Still the Judaizers demanded, "You can't be saved without being circumcised." After years of unrest, Paul took the problem to the apostles in Jerusalem for their answer.

How long the council lasted isn't recorded. We do know it was peppered with debates and strong arguments (Acts 15:2, 7). Again, the Judaizers refused to give one inch. "Let them be circumcised or they can't be saved." Two things are glaringly obvious: these Judaizers didn't mention what customs the women had to observe in order to be saved, and the apostles had no quick, ready answers.

Finally, after serious fasting and prayer by the apostles, the Spirit spoke, freeing the gentile Christians from all Jewish traditions. Reaching way back beyond Moses' law and Sinai, the Spirit of God said, "Abstain from things sacrificed to idols and from blood, and from things strangled and from fornication; if you keep yourselves free from such things, you will do well" (Acts 15:29). This command forever released all non-Jewish believers from observing Mosaic customs and ordinances.

From that time on there were two branches of the Christian church, the Jewish church and the gentile church. Unfortunately, the Judaizers disappeared shortly after the Roman armies of Titus destroyed the Temple and Jersualem in A.D. 70.

The Duration of the Law

The law was "added because of the transgressions, having been ordained through angels by the agency of a mediator, until the Seed should come to whom the promise had been made" (Gal. 3:19). We know that Christ was the Seed; therefore, the law lasted until He came; then it was canceled and put away. Since that time, the law has had no final authority over New Covenant believers. Paul also said the law was a tutor exposing our sins and driving us to Christ, but after receiving faith in Christ, the tutor isn't necessary any longer. Now there is "neither Jew nor Greek, there is neither slave nor free, there is neither male nor female; for you are all one in Christ Jesus" (Gal. 3:28 RSV; c.f. Col. 3:11).

Did the first apostolic council's decision, inspired and established by the Spirit of God, satisfy the Judaizers? Apparently not! Even though they were believers, they persisted in doing their own thing. Some time later, Sosthenes, the leader of the synagogue in Corinth, was beaten by the Jews in front of the judgment seat (Acts 18:17). Paul stayed with this dear brother while writing the Corinthian letter (1 Cor. 1:1).

One can only surmise why these Christian Jews refused to settle down and accept Paul's authority, but several observations can be stated. They were fanatically proud of their heritage and traditions, which the gentiles completely ignored. Evidently, the gentile believers had the power of God resting upon them and such gifted believers made the ungifted jealous. Then there was the explosive growth factor. Judaism, from its beginning, has never been an evangelistic movement, so its influence on outside societies was and is limited. But not so with the gentile believers. Connybeare and Howson, in their valuable *Life of St. Paul,* suggested that the Corinthian church may have had some 60,000 believers. And many of the converts were women, fresh from the pagan temples and Jewish synagogues. They were liberated women who enjoyed their new freedom in Christ since there were no spiritual distinctions between them and the male believers (Gal. 3:28).

Undoubtedly the outspoken women, in direct contradiction to and violation of the Jewish traditions, disturbed the Judaizers. While the uncircumcised males provoked a boisterous argument, the scandal of women speaking publicly was considered deplorable. And in the forefront was Priscilla, who worked alongside Paul as his contemporary and exercised her teaching gift and ministry freely.

Dean Alford, an Anglican scholar during the nineteenth century, said, "Aquila was a ready and zealous patron rather than a teacher. Priscilla had the gift and her husband gave her the support."[9] W.H. Ramsay, who researched and wrote *The Church In The Roman Empire,* said, "In Asia Minor, women had equality with men. During this period Roman woman were elevated to full and equal status without any distinction between the sexes." We can assume that when Priscilla came to Corinth, a gentile metropolis, she continued in the same freedom she had in Pontus, the Roman province where she had met and married her husband, Aquila.[10]

Chapter One Notes

1. W.E. Vine, *Expository Dictionary of New Testament Words* (Old Tappan, NJ: Fleming H. Revell, 1966).
2. Susan Foh, *Women and the Word of God* (Phillipsburg, NJ: Presbyterian and Reformed Publishing Co., 1979), p. 121.
3. *Mishnah Midoth* 2, 5.
4. *Midoth*, 2.
5. Josephus, *Antiquities XV.*
6. *Babylonian Talmud, Kiddushin*, 29B.
7. *Mishnah Sotah*, 3, 4.
8. *Babylonian Talmud, Kiddyshin*, 70A.
9. Katherine Bushnell, *God's Word to Women* (1923; privately reprinted by Ray Munson, N. Collins, NY).
10. See also J. Balsdon, *Roman Women, Their History and Habits* (London: 1962).

2

Paul's Contradictions

> Every man who has something on his head while praying or prophesying, disgraces his head. But every woman who has her head uncovered while praying or prophesying, disgraces her head . . . (1 Cor. 11:4, 5 NAS).

If Paul meant silence as traditionally interpreted, why did he contradict himself by saying women may pray and prophesy? And why would he equate the woman's ministry with the man's in the same statement? Context demands that just as the man prays and prophesies, the woman also prays and prophesies. Neither one is silent. Or does the man speak loud enough to be heard while the woman speaks to herself? Consistency and context demand that whatever the man is doing, the woman is doing the same thing. Paul used one to contrast and compare with the other.

Would the apostle permit the women to pray and prophesy in chapter 11:5 and then reverse himself and tell them to be silent in chapter 14:34-35?

Was he confused? Contradictory? No more so than the traditionalists who try to unravel this obvious mystery and still hang onto their sacred historical positions that all women must be silent. Here are some of their explanations.

1. Some say this was a particular local problem so it doesn't concern us. "But if one is inclined to be contentious, we have no other practice, nor have the churches of God" (1 Cor. 11:16). This explanation is based on the fact that we're living in a vastly different age with diverse social conditions, and concludes that Paul's order doesn't apply to us.

2. When confronted with the statements "woman may pray and prophesy" and "let your women be silent," some say Paul changed his mind. Frankly, this flimsy excuse is hardly acceptable. If Paul was inspired and Spirit-led, and if all Scripture is given by God, who changed Paul's mind? Who inspired him? Sorry, folks. If this reasoning is valid, we can't trust anything Paul said about anything. Was his writing in 1 Corinthians inspired or wasn't it?

3. Others, rather than examining what Paul really said, justify the contradiction by saying, "In those days, as in the Jewish synagogue, the women sat on one side and talked to the men on the other side, causing confusion." This explanation, already touched on in chapter one, is unacceptable on at least two counts.

First, the Corinthian church was made up almost entirely of gentile converts. There were some Jews but the majority of the believers were gentiles. Why would Paul use Jewish traditions and customs as guidelines for the Christian church after the Jerusalem council excused them from these traditions? Second, there isn't any historical evidence for this statement. I realize how deeply entrenched some Judaeo-Christian traditions can be, but is the Church built on tradition or fact? On human interpretations or truth? Inspired by God or man's ideas about God? I am not persuaded by the argument that these women were boorish and acted like mouthy children.

4. Another explanation offered is a little more reasonable: "Paul only forbade wives to ask questions during the services." But why silence just the married women? Were they the only ones talking, and if so, why?

Trombley's Explanation

Since everyone has a private interpretation, I *had* mine. I knew the context of 1 Corinthians 14: prophesying. So this passage must fit into that context. "You all [both men and women] may prophesy." I knew it included women since Paul's previous statement in 11:4 established that, but how do verses 34 and 35 fit into this context?

I assumed the word *gunaikes* meant "married woman," because I hadn't taken the time to check for myself, and some reputable books state it as fact. Neither *gune* or *aner* always means married woman or man. In Acts 8:27 the Ethiopian eunuch was an *aner,* but he wasn't married. Likewise, in Acts 10:30, Cornelius was visited by an angel, an *aner,* but angels aren't married. Therefore, the context of the passage determines the correct translation.

Paul told the prophets to judge all prophecies (1 Cor. 14:29). All may prophesy, so all may learn and be exhorted. From this context of the order for speaking in tongues and for prophesying and judging prophecy, he jumped directly into verses 34 and 35, the passage we're unraveling. Since the overall subject is judging prophecy, I assumed the silencing of women (wives) to be in this context. In other words, the prophets' wives must be silent. "Don't ask your prophet husbands questions during the time he's judging prophecy. If you have any questions ask him at home. Don't cause confusion during the service." I taught this interpretation for many years, and others accepted and used it, and quite frankly, I think it's as acceptable as most, but there was always one nagging question.

Where Does the Law Tell Women to be Silent and Why?

Where in all the Scriptures, except this one verse which appeals to a law, is there a suggestion that it's a shame for a woman to speak? Shelves of commentaries in public libraries left me bleary-eyed and nothing new was uncovered. Dick Mills had his research staff photocopy pages from 114 commentaries, one of them dating back to 1645, and they all said the same thing. There were references to Genesis 2 and 3 when commentary authors were appealing to the order of creation, but I found nothing that hinted, either directly or indirectly, of the shamefulness of women speaking in public. I realize these ancient scholars had church tradition and opinion over the centuries on their side, but I failed to see the thrust of their teaching in these commentaries. Some said Genesis 3:16 is the passage where God cursed woman and silencing was part of that curse.

These two chapters in Genesis, one dealing with the creation of mankind, the other with mankind's fall and its horrible result, are the only two references given where man was elevated as woman's guardian and ruler because God supposedly cursed her.

A popular radio teacher said it like this: "Created for the man, the woman was made subordinate to him from the very first; but the supremacy of the man was not intended to become a despotic rule . . . but in the fall that's what it becomes."[1] In other words, God designated man as the undisputed leader of the family when He "cursed" the woman in Genesis 3:16. Society didn't assign the position of authority to man; he was divinely appointed the family head by God, according to Dr. MacArthur.

If the Scriptures do say this, what does it have to do with the women being silent in the church. How does the family setting become the church setting? Further, nothing is said to suggest that women's talking is shameful.

18

Did God Curse Eve?

This question is fully answered in chapter eleven, but a brief preview is in order at this time. When God said, "Your desire will be for your husband and he will rule you" (Gen. 3:16), He didn't curse her again, did He? Paul said the curse of sin is death (Gal. 3:13).

God warned man what would happen if he sinned. "In the day you eat of it you shall surely die!" The punishment would be death, nothing more, nothing less, since God meant exactly what He said. Death was the punishment for sin and Paul called it the curse. Did God add an additional "curse" just for women?

Without doubt God cursed the serpent and the ground because of Adam, but nowhere does the passage say or imply He cursed either the man or woman. He did tell them what would happen because of their sin. God's statement wasn't in the form of a command but a dire warning!

He didn't say, "You *must* earn your bread by the sweat of your brow" as a command but as a statement of fact, "You *will!*" He didn't say, "You *must* bear children with pain," but "You *will!*" In other words, these will be the consequences of your sin. The reason is this: scholars say the verb form is the simple imperfect, which usually translates into the English as a future tense. If this statement were a command it would be in the imperative form. Rather than God "cursing" them, He warned them, prophetically telling them how it would be. He knew Adam's fallen nature would make him a tyrant. He knew he would abuse and use the woman, eventually reducing her to the position of common property. It wasn't God's desire; it was the terrible result of sin. Not a curse, but a consequence.

Had the imperative form been used, the meaning would be a direct command and man would have to dominate the woman in order to fulfill the command. The more carnal and violent the man, the more perfectly he would fulfill this order, but thank God that wasn't the situation at all. The verb is in the simple imperfect form, warning them what would happen.[2] Did God curse woman? Absolutely not! Did He curse man? Absolutely not!

The other passage the commentators refer to is Genesis 2:23: "She shall be called Woman, Because she was taken out of Man." The commentators claim that since man was created first, he has the primal right of authority. It's implied, they say, in God's statement that man needed a helper. Since she helps the man, her position is one of following or taking orders. Or as MacArthur wrote, "God designed someone to be in charge, and someone to help; someone to be in authority, and someone to be submissive; someone to be the leader, and someone to be the follower; someone to take care of the provisions, and someone to be provided for."[3] How did he reach his conclusion? Where does the Bible say anything about primal right and where does it say the first is better and the last is lesser? Nevertheless, this is where Paul supposedly got his apostolic authority for headship and man's dominion over women, including her being silenced in church.

*What Is the Law That Demands
the Obedient Silence of Women?*

Since "the law" is the authority appealed to by I Corinthians 14:34, 35 for subjugating women, it must be found. Generations of Christian women have lived under a heavy mountain of guilt because of these two verses. Attempts to placate them with flip answers such as "Woman is equal with man, but she must obey him" are neither satisfactory nor logical. Was Paul revealing the mind of the exalted Christ or was he quoting someone else in the church? Was this another one of the questions the Corinthians asked him to answer?

Chapter Two notes

1. John MacArthur, *Family Feuding and How to End It* (Panorama City, CA: Word of Grace Communications, 1981), p. 34.
2. Katherine Bushnell, *God's Word to Women* (1923, privately reprinted by Ray Munson, N. Collins, NY), p. 127.
3. John MacArthur, op. cit., p. 37.

3

As Also Saith the Law

J.F. Schleusner, the German lexicographer, stated: "The expression 'as also saith the law' refers to the Oral Law of the Jews now called the Talmud."[1] He also quoted Vitringa, an ancient Jewish scholar, who said women were excluded from the synagogue "not only from teaching but also from learning, by a very bad custom."

The late Katherine Bushnell, M.D., Hebrew and Greek scholar, researched and wrote *God's Word to Women* during the nineteenth century. She lived in London where she had access to some of the finest libraries in existence. Several times in her book, which is a series of 100 Bible studies, she referred to the law as being the oral law of the Jews.

During my initial study of this vital subject I shared some of my research findings on the *PTL* television program. A short time later I received a gracious letter from a lady in Pennsylvania and a gift copy of *Women In Judaism* by Leonard Swidler.[2] Dr. Swidler's book is a thorough examination of the status of women in Israel during formative Judaism and continuing well into the Common Era. His work is the result of endless hours exploring the Talmud and related

23

Jewish writings. Dr. Swidler's book pointed me in the right direction. If any reader is interested in a complete, well-documented thesis on the status of women in Judaism, this is the best, if not the only, sourcebook available.

What Were the Traditions Jesus Renounced?

What did the Lord have in mind when He said, "You transgress the commandment of God for the sake of your tradition?" (Matt. 15:3 NAS). In Mark 7:3 we read about the Pharisees carefully washing their hands, observing the traditions of the elders, and Jesus rebuking them by saying, "Neglecting the commandment of God, you hold to the tradition of men."

These traditions refer to the regulations handed down orally from one generation to another; they formed the oral law of the Jews. Those laws are now called the Talmud, an Aramaic word meaning "learning." They are a collection of the discussions, decisions, sayings and interpretations of the early scribes and rabbis, who were called Tannaim, on how to live according to the Torah, the law.

These teachings and traditions gradually became law, *halacha,* and were accepted to be as authoritative as the written Word. That's why Jesus rebuked the Pharisees when their traditions directly contradicted the Word itself. The main body, written in Hebrew and called the *Mishnah,* is a commentary on the Torah, while the Aramaic *Gemara* is a collection of additional discussions and commentaries on what the Mishnah really means.

The Babylonian Talmud is a collection of comments on the Mishnah by later rabbis, who were called Amoraim. There is also the Palestinian Talmud, and the Tosephta, Mechilta, Sifre and Sifra Scripture commentaries, which are mostly materials from the Tannaim and the early Midrash (the rabbinic stories illustrating the Torah).

The Mishnah is divided into six orders, or sedarim, and comprises sixty-three tractates, of which only thirty-six and one-half have a Gemara. There are six tractates specifically dealing with women as sisters-in-law, with betrothals and with the menstruants. For centuries the oral law was passed from generation to generation by word of mouth until it was codified or committed to writing in the second century C.E.; those who believe it contains the oral law given to Moses on Sinai consider it as authoritative as the Scriptures.

How the Oral Law Began and Why

Before we begin our search into this law to see what it has to say about women, a word should be said about the authority the scribes, later called rabbis, held in early Judaism.

During the long Babylonian exile, the Israelites lost their native tongue as a common language and they gradually accepted Aramaic, a common commercial language. Their Temple was gone, their religious rituals were not practiced and their priesthood was without a place to function, so synagogues were organized as places to pray, but not to replace the Temple or the priesthood. During seventy years as slaves in a pagan society, their unique religious heritage faded. Pagan practices and philosophies were adapted for daily Jewish life. Less and less they lived as Jews and more and more they lived by the culture of Babylon.

During the captivity, one group of men cared for the temple archives, especially the scrolls of the law. At first they were called scribes. Ezra, the first of this order, is credited with establishing the first rabbinical schools (Ezra 7:6, 11; Neh. 8:1; 12:26). Since Hebrew had almost disappeared from daily use, someone was needed to interpret the Hebrew Scriptures and explain their meaning. The scribes filled that need, reading the law in Hebrew and then explaining it to the people in Aramaic. The laymen depended entirely on these men for their knowledge of what the Word of God actually said and meant. Naturally, as time went by, the scribes received great respect and what they said became *halacha,* or law.

When the captivity ended, much had changed in the societies around Israel. As early as the ninth century B.C.E., Greek society had begun accepting women, slaves and children as individuals of worth rather than as inferior beings. Consequently, polygamy was abandoned and marital fidelity became the new ethic. In the fourth century B.C.E., Athens gave birth to what later was called Hellenism, a social system that was sensitive to human needs. When Alexander the Great set out to conquer the world, he also desired to spread this Greek culture. His success influenced the ancient Near East, changing it as drastically as the industrial revolution changed the agrarian society of early America. This new culture with its liberal ideals was shockingly different from the rigid Jewish lifestyle known before the exile. It must be remembered that the Jewish society had been founded on the patriarchal or tribal system where preference was alwas given to males. The Jews still practiced polygamy and regarded slaves and women as property rather than as equals.

The growth of any culture depends on education. Hellenism allowed women to receive an education; Judaism did not. Hellenist husbands were severely penalized for marital infidelity; the Jews considered infidelity a sin against a man's property, not a moral problem. Non-Jewish women could inherit property; Jewish women could not. Marriage under Hellenism was a joining of two equals, while Jews still bought and sold their wives. Women under Hellenism were able to participate fully in their religous rites; Jewish women were for the most part excluded. Hellenist women participated in sports, the arts and social life. A Jewish man had exclusive conjugal power over his wife; she couldn't divorce him, but he could divorce her. She couldn't have more than one husband, while he practiced polygamy. She couldn't inherit or own property, but her husband could. She had absolutely no voice in her marriage, whom she would marry, when or why; it was exclusively the decision of her father and the man he bargained with.

When Roman culture supplanted Greek civilization, the Hellenistic principles were retained. Early Roman society, like most primitive cultures, did little to improve the daily lives of women. But by the third century B.C.E., the situation began improving. Women married by their own choice, could divorce their husbands if necessary and even chose their own name.[3] No longer were women subject to the sovereign authority of the patriarchal heads, neither did men have total conjugal power over their wives.

Meanwhile, Jewish leaders tried to cling to the ancient tribal system where men were supreme and women were considered property. However, the new family structure was founded on individual and personal ties, and the patriarchal family organization began to fade away. Consequently, the world and society fearfully challenged Judaism during and after their seventy-year captivity. The Jews lost their identity, their Temple, their tongue, their nation, and their family structure, but not their law.

In the fifth century B.C.E., Ezra, a skilled scribe in the law of Moses, discovered that the Jews of Jerusalem, including some priests, had married non-Jewish wives, contrary to Moses' law of separation. If the practice had continued, Jewish culture might have been lost forever, so Ezra ordered them to divorce these women (Ezra 9, 10). Thirteen years later, after Nehemiah had repaired the broken walls of Jerusalem, Ezra and the other priests and Levites read from the law of God, translating it to give the sense so that the people understood the reading. Few still understood the now little-used language of Hebrew, making it necessary for the scribes to explain what they read (Neh. 8:8). The actions of these zealous men were the beginnings of formative Judaism. Their original purpose was noble. Their successors in the succeeding centuries saw the Hellenistic invasion as a threat to preservation of pre-exilic Judaism and they wanted to maintain their unique identity. It wasn't long before the unlearned people looked upon them as possessing special knowledge and spiritual illumination. Since the priests and scribes explained the written law, their words soon became law. Gradually the Scriptures were reduced to a maze of rules, regulations and traditions, many of them contradictory. The rabbis, the oral law, and customs replaced God's Word. By the time Jesus began His ministry these *halacha* had become the traditions which made null and void the commandments of God. They were the same Jewish fables Paul resisted.

The Oral Law and Women

According to the Bible and history, women fared much better before the exile. However, the Talmud reveals a steady decline in the status of women's freedom after the return from Babylon. It is my purpose to follow that trail of repression into the New Testament era and the beginnings of the Christian church. I'm aware that a short thesis can't possibly give all the available information, but we'll explore three main areas where the Talmud is explicit: the religious, social, and marital status of women, including education, the study of the Torah, and women in the Temple and synagogue. It is my intention to present this material in such a way that it speaks for itself and that when we're finished you'll understand what the Corinthian Judaizers meant when they said, "as also saith the law."

The Jewish Attitude Toward Women

All Jewish males prayed a prescribed daily thanksgiving which accurately describes their opinion of women:

Praise be to God he has not created me a Gentile; praise be to God that he has not created me a woman; praise be to God that he has not created me an ignorant man.[4]

One of the gravest insults was to call a Jewish man a gentile, a slave, or a fool. These three groups of humans had the lowest status possible. By equating women with them, the men revealed what was in their hearts. They thanked God daily for not being women. Lest one of my readers dismiss this daily prayer (still prayed by ultra-orthodox Jews) as an isolated text, it's repeated in at least three of the ancient Mishnahs: the *Tosephta Berakhoth* 7, 8; the *Palestinian Talmud Berakhoth* 13b; and the *Babylonian Talmud Menakhoth* 43b. Josephus, a well-known Jewish historian who said he was a Pharisee, wrote, "The woman, says the law, is in all things inferior to the man. Let her accordingly be submissive."[5] He referred to the oral law, not the Bible, as "the law." It's the same law referred to in 1 Corinthians 14:34-35. All Jewish regulations for the submission of women are based on ancient sources in the Mishnahs and not on the Bible. This basic concept is important since male dominance of women is based on it. "Adam was the light of the world and Eve was the cause of his death; therefore, she has been given the precept about lighting the sabbath lamp." "Concerning menstruation: the first man was the blood and life of the world . . . and Eve was the cause of his death; therefore, she has been given the menstruation precept."[6] These interpretations, comments and ideas are the personal opinions of the rabbis and not the Word of God. They are not the way the Bible should be interpreted.

This degrading of all women is based on the teachers' faulty concept of the Fall. The Babylonian Talmud lists the "Ten Curses God Uttered Against Eve."[7] Due to their explicit nature, I'll only outline them here.[8]

1. "greatly multiply" deals with woman's menstrual curse;

2. "Thy sorrow" is having and rearing children;

3. "Thy conception" shall be by the husband's choice and at his discretion;

4. "in sorrow thou shall bring forth children" is more punishment of women;

5. "thy desire shall be unto thy husband" deals with the rabbis' private interpretation of sexuality;

6. "he shall rule over thee," the wife being in total submission and subjugation, since the wife is the personal property of the husband;

7. "she is wrapped up like a mourner," that is,

8. "she shall not appear in public with her head uncovered";

9. "she is restricted to one husband" while the husband may have many wives;

10. "she is confined to the house."

I'm quite convinced that if the full extent of these rabbinical curses were known, many Christian churches would have second thoughts before embracing them. In fact, the idea that God cursed woman is strictly a rabbinical idea based on a very wrong premise. Paul's epistle to the Romans emphatically states that sin *did not* come into the world through Eve but through Adam. It was the oral law, not the Old or New Testament, which wrongly accused Eve of being the cause of Adam's sin and death.

Judaism had a double standard regarding Jewish women. In John 8:1-11 the Pharisees dragged a woman before Jesus demanding that He condemn her *according to their oral law.*

"Teacher, this woman has been caught in adultery, in the very act." If she was caught in the act there must have been a man with her. Why wasn't he condemned also? Because of the double standard and misinterpretation of Scripture. What was sin for the woman wasn't sin for the man. Apparently this woman wasn't married or the man might have been judged with her, because he would have violated another man's property rights: women were considered chattels along with slaves, houses, land and animals. A wife was her husband's exclusive property. Committing adultery with a man's wife was the same as stealing his goat or using his horse without permission. A woman had no recourse even if a man infected her with venereal disease or inflicted brutality on her. The rabbis, however, would have argued that they had a scriptural basis for their *halacha.* The tenth commandment says: "Thou shalt not covet thy neighbour's wife . . . nor his ox, nor his ass" (KJV). From that statement the rabbis concluded that wives were classified with animals and other property.

As long as a man wasn't caught with another man's wife he wasn't sinning, but adultery was always a sin for a woman regardless of the circumstances. That's why they brought the woman but not the man to Jesus for His judgment, and that's why He reacted violently to their hypocrisy. Rebuking their false doctrine He said, "He who is without sin among you, let him be the first to throw a stone at her."

Men divorced their wives at will, but under no circumstances could a wife divorce her husband.[9] Only men spoke in public.[10] No woman could give a testimony or conduct business.[11] Generally, the attitude toward women was one of disregard, subjugation and repression.[12] Here are a few rabbinical statements displaying their attitude:

"A woman is a pitcher full of filth with its mouth full of blood, yet all run after her."[13] "When a boy comes into the world, peace comes into the world; when a girl comes, nothing comes."[14] "At the birth of a boy all are joyful, but at the birth of a girl all are sad."[15] "She is greedy, eavesdropping, slothful, and envious." "She is also a scratcher and talkative." "She is also

31

prone to steal and is a gadabout."[16] "Our teachers have said: 'Four qualities are evident in women: they are greedy at their food, eager to gossip, lazy and jealous.' "[17] What can one conclude except that there was distasteful bigotry or outright ignorance regarding women?

Jewish women were to be seen as little as possible and heard even less. Young men were warned not to talk to or get involved with them since it would take their minds off their study of the law. A century before Christ, Rabbi Johanan warned that a man should not "talk not much with womankind, even his wife, even his sister." "He that talks much with womankind brings evil upon himself and neglects the study of the Law and at the last will inherit Gehenna."[18] During prayer and Torah study, men were urged to avoid any contact with women, including their own wives.[19] Serious students of the law were allowed to sexually deny their wives for as long as three years. One rabbi permitted twelve years.[20]

Women were not required to know or fulfill the law. One rabbi unmistakably spelled it out: "Because she has a single heart toward her husband; likewise the heart of the slave is directed to his master . . . Women and slaves still have a human master over them and the service of him makes such a claim on their heart that the time and energy for the service of God is lacking. Therefore, a lesser claim in regard to fulfillment of the commandments is made on women and slaves than on men and freedom." "Women, slaves, and minors are exempt from the Sukkah."[21] Throughout the Mishnahs and Talmud, women, children, slaves and imbeciles are linked together and exempted from knowing or fulfilling the law since they are all subordinate to their masters.

Some rabbis exempted women from praying after meals. The saying of prayers was an important ritual with the Jews, and the exemption of women, slaves and children illustrates again their lower status and worth. Some rabbis excused them from saying the morning prayers, grace at meals and reciting the Shema (Deut. 6:4-9).[22] "A curse light on the man whose wife and children have to say grace for him."[23] Yet one *Mishnah* contradicts it by saying, "Women, slaves, or minors are not exempt from saying the prayers after meals."[24] Still, both contradictions are *halacha*—law. This explains why the Jews often asked Jesus who was right, Hillel or Shammai?

Included in the male Jewish attitude toward women was the threat: "For three transgressions do women die in childbirth: for heedlessness of the laws concerning menstruation, the dough-offering, and the lighting of the Sabbath lamp."[25] Menstruation was part of the curse all women supposedly suffer because Eve shed Adam's blood. Adam was considered the pure Hallah (leaven) for the world; Eve, supposedly having caused his death, is forever required to make the dough-offering. The "light precept" was given because she "extinguished Adam's light by causing his death."[26] Throughout the Talmud, the rabbis constantly blamed sin, death and suffering on Eve and this blame gave them reason for debasing women. This is undoubtedly the reason Paul covered the subject thoroughly in his Roman epistle. "By one man sin entered into the world" (Rom. 5:12 KJV). In verse 12, rather than the word *anthropon,* meaning a human being, Paul used the masculine "one." By implicating Adam as the originator of sin, he eliminated the grounds for subjugating women as part of Eve's curse.

Women Studying the Law

Only the rabbis knew the Hebrew language and the law of Moses, and they refused to teach women. An article under "Education" in the *Encyclopaedia Judaica* states: "There was general agreement that a woman was not obliged to study Torah. As a result few were learned . . . If a woman didn't study Torah, they weren't educated." The *Babylonian Talmud* states, "He who is not versed in the Scriptures and the Mishnah and in good conduct is of no benefit to the public weal."[27] In other words, since women weren't educated in the Torah or expected to fulfill it, they were valueless to Judaism.

Several rabbis refused to let women function in any part of Jewish society. Rabbi Eliezar, a first-century teacher, passed along what he had learned in a long, unbroken chain of tradition: "Rather should the words of the Torah be burned than entrusted to a woman . . . Whoever teaches his daughter the Torah is like one who teaches her obscenity."[28] Continuing, he said, "May the words of the Torah be burned rather than given to women."

Since the rabbis were the Hebrew scholars, they were the only ones who taught the Torah. Their attitude toward women as sex objects bears on the issue. If a woman wasn't physically attractive she was regarded poorly.[29] One rabbi plainly said, "A woman's leg is a sexual excitement. A woman's voice is a sexual excitement. If one gazes at the little finger of a woman, it is as if he gazes at her secret place."[30] Another stated, "A harsh voice is a bodily defect."[31] Rabbi Aha said, "He who gazes at a woman will eventually come to sin." Ben Sira, an outspoken and influential rabbi, said, "All women are nymphomaniacs" and "Do not converse much with women, as this will ultimately lead you to unchastity."[32] The same portion of the Talmud quotes another rabbi who said children are born "dead, because they converse during cohabitation; blind, because they look at 'that place.' "

Segregation in the Temple and Synagogue

Jewish women were completely separated from their husbands in both the Temple and synagogue. Herod's Temple, the one Jesus frequented, was specifically built for the separation of women and gentiles.

According to Josephus, the women entered the first court,

the court of the gentiles, and went to the court directly above that, the women's court. It was five steps above the gentile court but still fifteen steps below the men's court.[33] The court of the women was free of buildings and surrounded with a gallery so that the women should not mingle with the men. They had their own gates through which they entered the Temple. They were forbidden to enter the place within seven days of their menstruation, or forty days of the birth of a boy, or eighty days of the birth of a girl.[34] Separation was the premise on which the Temple was constructed, making a clear distinction between man and God, Jew and gentile, male and female, priest and people.

Archaeological research and data bear out this distinction: the remains of ancient synagogues in Galilee show the galleries, although some scholars deny that these galleries were for women since women were excluded from any active role in public worship.

One fact emerges: Jewish women never asked their husbands questions in public. In the Temple they did not sit opposite them; they were segregated some fifteen steps below them. They were silenced "as also saith the Law."

Women in Public

Jewish women stayed off the streets. "A woman should not show herself off like a vagrant in the streets before the eyes of other men, except when she has to go to the temple, and even then she should take pains to go, not when the market is full but when most people have gone home."[35] Any woman who ventured out with her hair unbound, spun in the street, or talked with other men set herself up for immediate divorce.

When she did go out she always had her head covered, because of the curses God supposedly spoke to Eve. Women undoubtedly wore the same covering in and around their homes although the custom wasn't rigidly followed in the rural areas.[36]

Some scholars suggest that single women were exempt from the covering, but this idea runs into Talmudic problems since all girls were to be married by age thirteen. Any girl who wasn't married when she reached puberty "ran the risk of becoming a whore."[37] In fact, rabbis demanded that both men and women marry. The men "because their time would be spent with sinful thoughts . . . but as soon as he marries his sins are stopped up."[38] Contrast this with the apostle Paul's statement that "it is good for a man not to touch a woman" (1 Cor. 7:1 KJV) or his advice to the unmarried women that it's better to remain single. The possibility of any Jewish girl beyond the age of twelve or thirteen walking about with her head uncovered was very slight. From a number of Talmudic references we can determine accurately what the head covering was.

A woman's hair was uncut and long. She braided it with two or more kerchiefs, which hung down to her shoulders. On her forehead she wore a headband of ribbons which hung down to her chin, and on top of this a hairnet, also tied together with ribbons and bows. This coiffure completely covered her face except for one eye, which was often painted.[39] One rabbi told a story about Tamar to illustrate how this custom originated: "Every bride who is modest in the house of her father-in-law is rewarded by having kings and prophets among her descendants. How do we prove this? From Tamar, it is written . . . because she has covered her face in the house of her father-in-law and he did not know her, she was rewarded."[40]

As with all Talmudic regulations, this practice was based on the Scriptures. Numbers 5:16-23 gives the ritual for serving the "waters of bitterness," an ancient custom to test whether a woman (never a man) was guilty of adultery. The priest made the woman stand before the Lord, her head uncovered, her hair loose. From this Scripture the requirement for a head covering developed as interpreted by the rabbis.

The reason behind the covering is clearly spelled out. "And why does a man go out bareheaded while a woman goes out with her head covered? She is like one who has done wrong and is ashamed of people; therefore, she goes out with her head covered."[41]

Marriage, Divorce and the Torah

A young girl's destiny was controlled by her father until she was given away in marriage. She had no say in the matter; she was not consulted in any decision concerning her life. "The man may sell his daughter, but never the mother."[42] A woman was human property.

"The woman is acquired by three means and she regains her freedom by two methods. She is acquired by money, or by document, or by sexual intercourse. And she recovers her freedom by a letter of divorce or on the death of her husband."[43]

Long before the birth of rabbinicism men were urged to divorce "bad wives," although women could never divorce bad husbands. "Woman is the origin of sin and it is through her that we all die. If she does not accept your control, divorce her and send her away" (Sir. 25:25). Sirach is one of the apocryphal books of wisdom literature written during the second century B.C.E..

Most of the reasons for divorce were frivolous. If a woman ate in the street, drank greedily in the street, or suckled her baby in the street, she could be divorced. If she gossiped, spun in the moonlight, left her hair unfastened, spun in the street with her armpits uncovered, or bathed in the same place as men, she could be divorced. If she was childless for a ten-year period her husband could put her away.

Despite all the so-called religious grounds for divorce, Jesus summed them up in one simple but clear statement: "Because of your hardness of heart, Moses permitted you to divorce your wives; but from the beginning it has not been this way" (Matt. 19:8). Hardness of heart is insensitivity to the feelings of others, the trampling under foot of their rights and needs. From what the Talmud has revealed of the attitudes of Jewish men toward women, the Lord correctly summed up their terrible practices as hardness of heart.

However, there wasn't any way a woman could divorce her husband regardless of what he did to her. Male supremacy and the double standard still exist in some sects of Judaism today. *The Wichita Eagle Beacon* on October 1, 1983, carried an Associated Press article describing the injustices still practiced by the rabbis.

> When Heidi Stern's husband skipped to Mexico City he left her with two children, and a marriage she couldn't escape. Four years later, despite her civil divorce decree, she is still married in the eyes of her family, her friends, her community and her synagogue. Until her husband grants her a religious divorce, called a *get,* she cannot date other men, she cannot marry, and if she has any more children they will be labeled illegitimate. Heidi Stern is an *aqunah*—a chained woman.

She is one of several thousand Jewish women whose husbands have refused to dissolve their marriages *even though the man has remarried and begun another family.*

The *Beacon* article mentioned one college professor who spent fifteen days in jail when he refused an order by the State of New York to give his wife a religious divorce. He too has remarried. Under Jewish law, a divorce is valid only when a panel of three rabbis grants it. Until then she remains bound to her husband until he grants her a religious divorce, even though he has the privilege of remarrying. Once again, it is the woman who bears the brunt of man's injustice.

Polygamy was long a Jewish tradition, but polyandry (a woman having more than one husband at a time) was forbidden. "A woman is not eligible to two [men], but is not a man eligible to two women?"[44] The rabbis were for the most part monogamists; however, there were some who practiced polygamy. The son of Gamaliel was a member of the Sanhedrin who had two wives at one time.[45] Josephus, the historian and a Pharisee, claimed four wives, at least two of them at the same time. King Herod, builder of the great Temple, had ten wives, many of them at the same time.[46] Josephus wrote, "It is an ancestral custom of ours to have several wives at the same time."[47] Nor were these practices limited to the pre-Christian period. Late in the first century C.E., Rabbi Hananvah noted the polygamous marriages of several high-priestly families.[48] Please keep these facts in mind when reading Paul's qualifications for bishops and elders: "A bishop must be . . ." the husband of one wife (1 Tim. 3:1-13 KJV). It's apparent Paul wasn't talking about divorced people in the ministry but Jews with more than one wife.

Finally, something should be said about Judaism's problems with menstruation and the stigma it held. The Levitical law was explicit about all bodily discharges and uncleanness. Ritual purity was rigidly enforced since it was one of the steps to spiritual holiness (Lev. 15:1-33). For a priest to "render a knife impure was more serious than bloodshed."[49] "If a priest served in a state of uncleanness his brethren priests did not bring him to the court, but the young men among the priests took him outside the Temple Court and split open his brain with clubs."[50]

Death was the penalty for violating these purity laws. The *niddah,* the menstruant, was the subject of ten chapters in the part of the *halacha* dealing with purification laws. "If even a spot of blood as large as a mustard seed appeared" she was considered unclean for another seven days, during which time she could not enter either the temple or synagogue.[51] Consequently, many women were unclean most of the time. No one could eat with a woman during her uncleanness. She was excluded from her home and stayed in a special house known as the "house of uncleanness."[52]

Many if not all of these restrictions against women were begun during the first years after the return from the exile, during the beginning of formative Judaism. By the time the Common Era began, women were bound even further, until finally even her spittle or the dust of her feet made her husband unclean and restricted him from entering the Temple or synagogue.

This was the condition of women in Judaism when Christ came and a New Covenant was given. Talmudic or Rabbinical Judaism with its endless traditions, interpretations, customs and fables had negated the true meaning of God's Word. With the coming of the Messiah a new day dawned for men and women.

Chapter Three Notes

1. *The Tyro's Greek Lexicon* (London: Brown and Greek, 1825).
2. Leonard Swidler, *Women in Judaism* (Metuchen, NJ: Scarecrow Press, 1976).
3. John Baldson, *Roman Women, Their History and Habits* (Greenwood, 1975) in Swidler, *Women in Judaism*, p. 23.
4. *Tosephta Berakhoth* 7, 8.
5. Josephus, *Apion II*, 201.
6. *Tosephta Shabbath* 2, 10; *Palestinian Talmud Shabbath* 2, 5b, 34; *Babylonian Talmud Shabbath* 31b, 32a; Rabah 17, 18.
7. *Erubin*, 100b.
8. *Genesis With a Talmudic Commentary* by Herson lists the curses in detail.
9. *Babylonian Talmud, Kiddushin* 1, 11.
10. Ibid., *Berakhoth* 4, 36; *Mishnah Aboth* 1, 5.
11. *Mishnah Shabbath* 4, 1; Sifre D. 19:17.
12. *Tosephta Berakhoth* 7, 18.
13. *Babylonian Talmud, Shabbath* 152a.
14. Ibid., *Niddah* 31b.
15. Ibid.
16. Ibid.; *Midrashim Rabbah* 18, 2.
17. *Midrashim Rabbah* 45, 5.
18. *Mishnah Aboth* 1, 5.
19. *Babylonian Talmud, Kethuboth* 5, 6.
20. Ibid., 62b.
21. *Palestinian Talmud, Sukkah* 2, 7.
22. *Babylonian Mishnah, Berakhoth* 7, 2.
23. *Babylonian Talmud, Berakhoth* 20b.
24. *Mishnah Berakhoth* 3, 3.
25. *Mishnah Shabbath* 2, 6.
26. *Palestinian Talmud, Shabbath* 3, 5b, 34.

27. *Kiddushin*, 1, 10.
28. *Babylonian Talmud, Kiddushin*, 70a.
29. *Mishnah Kethuboth* 7, 7.
30. *Babylonian Talmud, Berakhoth* 24a; *Shabbath* 64b.
31. Ibid., *Kethuboth* 75a.
32. Ibid., *Ned* 20a.
33. Josephus, *Antiquities*, XV, 418f.
34. Josephus, *Apion II*, 103.
35. *Mishnah Kethuboth* 6, 6; *Babylonian Talmud, Gittin* 90a.
36. Leonard Swidler, *Biblical Affirmations of Woman* (Philadelphia: Westminster Press, 1979), p. 123.
37. *Babylonian Sanhedrin*, 76a.
38. *Babylonian Talmud, Kiddushim* 29b; *Babylonian Yebamoth* 63b.
39. *Mishnah Shabbath* 8, 3.
40. *Babylonian Talmud, Megilla* 10b.
41. *Midrashim Genesis Rabbah* 17, 7.
42. *Mishnah Sotah* 3, 8.
43. *Babylonian Talmud, Kiddushim* 1, 1.
44. Ibid., 7a.
45. *Babylonian Talmud, Yebamoth* 15a.
46. Josephus, *Antiquities, XIV* 300.
47. Ibid., *XVII*, 14.
48. *Babylonian Talmud, Yebamoth* 15b.
49. *Tosephta Yoma* 1, 12.
50. *Mishnah Sanhedrin* 9,6.
51. *Babylonian Talmud, Shabbath* 13a.
52. Ibid., *Niddah* 7, 4.

4

Paul's Answer to the Judaizers

From examining the Talmud, we can see that the rabbis were out of step, not only with the progressing civilizations around them, but also with their own Scriptures. The Roman, Egyptian and Hellenistic cultures had abandoned the ancient tribal practices of subjugating women. The primitive social structure in which males were always superior and females inferior had given way to the knowledge that women were human beings, with sensitive feelings and self-worth, fully capable of being a vital part of society. However, the Jews stuck to their tribal customs while the rabbis vainly tried to make them scriptural.

Rabbinical Commentaries as the Law

When a male Jew repented of his sins and crowned Jesus as both Lord and Christ, he became a new creature, and a participant in the New Covenant. However, most of them stayed within the framework of Judaism, keeping both the laws and customs. It was these Judaizers who insisted that the male gentiles must be circumcised and keep the customs of Moses. And these same Judaizers went after the Christian women.

"Let the women keep silent in the churches; for they are not permitted to speak, but let them subject themselves just as the Law also says" (1 Cor. 14:34).

There is a parallel between these ancient rabbis and the modern Iranian Muslims who refuse to enter the twentieth century, preferring to take their nation back to the seventh century and the birth of Islam in order to preserve their identity. Likewise, the purpose of rabbinicism was to make the Torah applicable to every area of life and preserve the ancient Hebrew heritage. These rabbis weren't Spirit-filled or Spirit-led men, so their personal bias, desires, prejudices, fears and ideas based on superstition and misinformation flavored everything they said. And what they said became *halacha,* law, which had to be obeyed. Their authority is still evident today. When Heidi Stern was asked whether she had considered dating or remarrying without her husband first giving her a religious divorce, she replied, "I would not break Jewish law any more than I would secular law."

The oral law wasn't inspired as was the Word of God any more than *Matthew Henry's Commentary* or the *Pulpit Commentary* is inspired. The oral law was made up of what the rabbis thought the Torah meant. They thought it said women were sexually seductive, mentally inferior, socially embarrassing, and spiritually separated from the law of Moses; therefore, let them be silent. It was the Jewish oral law, not the Bible, that demanded the silence of women. That law wasn't the original, inspired Word of God spoken through the mouth of holy men of God; it was Jewish traditionalism.

Paul's Answer

Sir William Ramsey, former professor at the University of Aberdeen in Glasgow, was widely known for his thorough research into the history of Christianity in Asia Minor. He said "We should be ready to suspect Paul is making a quotation from the letter addressed to him by the Corinthians whenever he alludes to their knowledge, or when any statement stands in marked contrast either with the immediate context or with Paul's known views."[1]

Notice that the two controversial verses we're studying stand in marked contrast with verses 30-39 as well as with Paul's views expressed in 1 Corinthians 11:5. He said "All may prophesy that all may learn," without any qualification as to whether men or women were prophesying. Then he abruptly, and totally out of context, dropped his teaching on spiritual gifts and tackled the question of women being silent. Because it is in such marked contrast, some commentators have deliberately rearranged the order of these verses and placed them after verses 39-40 so Paul's theme would be uninterrupted. However, these verses are exactly where the Holy Spirit inspired Paul to place them since they are directly related to the overall problem. The marked contrast separated them from Paul's views and teaching.

The apostle didn't say, "don't permit," but "it is not permitted," suggesting someone else was doing the forbidding. The "it" would be the law since it is the law that says women must remain silent. Nowhere does the Bible say it is a shame for a woman to speak; therefore, the "law" can't be the Bible. The other law, the oral law of the Jews, specifically directed women to remain silent.

Several good commentaries such as *The Pulpit Commentary* suggest that Paul was answering one of the questions the Corinthians asked him in their letter, and that verses 34 and 35 are one of those questions or statements. It might be paraphrased like this: "Paul, these Corinthian women are prophesying publicly, praying out loud, speaking in tongues. The oral law says it is shameful for a woman to speak in public. Tell them to be silent and stop this talking!"

These women were told to ask their husbands questions at

home. Is this a universal requirement? We know that some of these women had unbelieving husbands (1 Cor. 7:15-17). Would Paul knowingly have sent them back to unsaved husbands for spiritual knowledge? Would he deliberately have told those who were married to unbelieving Jews to ask them for teaching? What would they learn except Jewish traditions? Further, Jewish women were excluded from studying the Torah. Or was Paul only talking to those who had Christian husbands? If this was the situation, did it demand the silence of all women for all time?

"It is a shame for a woman to speak in church" (1 Cor. 14:35). Why? What is the scriptural or logical reasoning that makes their voices shameful? Again, we know this wasn't Paul's attitude since he already had said women may pray and prophesy. If women can pray and prophesy, why would it now be shameful for them to speak? When Paul said, "it is not permitted," "they are commanded," "it is improper," and "as also saith the law," he referred to the unscriptural statement made to him rather than to his personal opinions. He didn't say, "I forbid!" but rather "it is not permitted."

It's absurd to suggest Paul was reverting back to the Jewish traditions as his authority for governing the status of Christian women. He told the Galatians, "[In Christ] there is neither male nor female" (Gal. 3:28). One mark of truly Spirit-led persons is the consistency of their statements.

Later, Paul warned Titus to guard against "giving heed to Jewish fables, and commandments of men" (Tit. 1:14 KJV). He cautioned Timothy about those "desiring to be teachers of the law, without understanding either what they are saying or the things about which they make assertions" (1 Tim. 1:7 RSV). It's unsettling to think the apostle to the gentiles used Jewish rabbinicism to guide the Christian church and its conduct and discipline. It's upsetting to think he violated the conclusions of the first council in Jerusalem when it seemed

46

good to the Holy Spirit, the apostles and the elders not to lay the burden of Jewish traditions on converts (Acts 15:23-29). Could it be that the apostles and elders released the new believers from the other traditions but kept this one? If so, why wasn't it included in the message Paul carried back to the churches?

There is one other argument regarding these verses. Since they interrupt Paul's flow of thought and they contradict 1 Corinthians 11:5, could they be an insertion added by a copyist? The authorship of the letter to the Corinthians has never been in doubt but some do challenge this portion. However, all reputable manuscripts include it.

Those who accept 1 Corinthians 14:34-35 at the expense of 11:2-16 argue that it seems unnecessary for Paul to forbid a woman to prophesy bare-headed since in 1 Timothy 2:12 he barred women from speaking in church altogether.

Still another theory distinguishes between the two types of services alluded to in 1 Corinthians 14—one, a closed meeting where the Eucharist was served to baptized believers, and the other, an open meeting where unbelievers were allowed to be present (14:22-25). According to this explanation, Paul was concerned about women speaking during the open meeting. However, the New Testament does not differentiate between open or closed, public or private meetings. Nor is the word "unbeliever" the best translation for *idiotes.* "Ignorant" or "ungifted" is a much better choice of words.

Susan Foh, author of *Women and the Word of God,* wrote that the law "refers to the whole body of Old Testament laws concerning women, which were intended to teach the submission of the wife to her husband". She conceded that women may pray and prophesy as allowed by Paul's statement in 1 Corinthians 11:5. Nor did she claim that the silence has to be total. Otherwise women couldn't sing, read responsive readings or pray the Lord's prayer in church. She did limit the silencing of women to the requirements of the law and asking questions. Her conclusion is based on the assumption that woman was created to serve as a helper, that woman's position is always one of subjugation to man.

Just how women being created to serve men as helpers relates to ministry in church eludes me. Women must, Susah Foh insisted, subordinate themselves as the law demands, but she didn't state what the law says. "As the law also saith" refers to women asking questions, according to Ms. Foh. But she didn't quote one Old Testament passage that remotely supports her thesis. She gave absolutely no reason why women shouldn't ask questions; she even admitted that most instruction was a series of questions and answers.

When all the evidence is considered, it's apparent Paul quoted the Judaizers when he wrote, "As the law also saith." Nowhere does the Bible restrict women to a position where they can't ask questions. Nor can I find any place where it is shameful for them to speak publicly, in the Temple or in a Christian church. Nor can I find any illustrations in the Bible where women ever experienced this kind of bondage. However, there are literally dozens of Talmudic references that spell out in detail these exact requirements. The oral law of the Jews didn't mince words. The voice of a woman was a hateful sound! If any man taught his daughter the Torah it was as though he taught her lechery. Nor could a woman come forward to publicly read from the Torah. Women were passive listeners and never participants in the synagogue or Temple. "May the words of the Torah be burned rather than be given to women."

The same Judaizers who clamored for the circumcision of men also demanded the total obedience of Christian women to their Jewish customs, especially the total silence in public services.

Now notice Paul's explosion! "Was it from you that the Word of God first went forth? Or has it come to you only?"

(1 Cor. 14:36). He bluntly rejected their demands based on their conclusion that the oral law was equal with the Word of God and had to be obeyed. With no uncertain message he called their hand.

"If anyone thinks he is a prophet or spiritual, let him recognize that the things which I write to you are the Lord's commandment . . . Therefore, my brethren [including women (1 Cor. 11:5)], desire earnestly to prophesy, and do not forbid to speak in tongues" (1 Cor 14:37, 39). The content of the whole chapter is the balanced use of tongues and prophecy, functions enjoyed by both men and women. Someone in the congregation was telling the women to hush and subject themselves as the law also says. The women were not silent on the day of Pentecost when the Spirit was poured out; Mary, the Lord's earthly mother, also spoke in tongues.

Some commentators say Paul reprimanded the Corinthians for letting the women prophesy, speak in tongues and ask questions as part of the method of teaching. If this is true, which of Paul's statements is correct? ". . . every woman . . . praying or prophesying" or "Let the women keep silent"? To imply Paul changed his mind and came down hard on the women is groundless since he permitted both men and women to prophesy. If he was only challenging those women with husbands, what of those who were unmarried? The textual difficulties surrounding Paul's alleged contradictions are cleared up when this passage is seen as a restatement of the question asked of Paul in the letter sent to him.

What he said is this, "Is the Word labeled 'Men Only' or did it come to both men and women?" His advice is a direct revelation from the Lord rather than a quote from the endless traditions and contradictory opinions of the rabbis. Then he added, "But if anyone does not recognize this, he is not recognized" (1 Cor. 14:38). He continued, "Therefore"—meaning the following is based on the previous argument—"desire earnestly to prophesy, and do not forbid to speak in tongues." Or as Dr. Howard Ervin, Professor at Oral Roberts University, put it, "You who are forbidding speaking in tongues . . . stop it!"

The Greek verb *koluo* also means "to hinder or restrain" as in Matthew 19:14: "Let the children alone, and do not hinder [*holuo*] them from coming to Me . . ." The same verb is used in 1 Thessalonians 2:16 where Paul described how the Jews tried to forbid or hinder him from speaking to the gentiles so they might be saved. In like manner, these same Judaizers hindered the Corinthians, including the women, from prophesying and speaking in tongues. His final word? "Stop it!"

Chapter Four Notes

1. Katherine Bushnell, *God's Word to Women* (1923; privately reprinted by Ray Munson, N. Collins, NY), para. 205.

5

Can Women Teach Publicly?

Are Women Restricted to Teaching
Children and Other Women?

This gets near the heart of the question. Can women teach? Most traditionalists soften their objections by granting women the privilege of singing or of teaching children and other women except when adult men are present. Of course there are various shades of liberalism, so no one position can be stated. Even though these modifications are concessionary, they are necessary if the denominations expect many women to stay in their churches. Are women scripturally restricted to teaching children and other women? If a woman teaches a boys' class, when do they enter manhood, and when does her ministry to them cease? Does the restriction apply to mothers teaching their sons?

The words "teach" and "teacher" appear more than 119 times in the Greek Scriptures but only one of them forbids women teaching. "But I do not allow a woman to teach or exercise authority over a man, but to remain quiet" (1 Tim. 2:12). This passage will be analyzed in depth in chapter sixteen. Is there any scripture where Paul allows women to teach? There is!

What Is Prophecy?

"But every woman . . . praying or prophesying . . ."(1 Cor. 11:5). In 1 Corinthians 14:3 prophecy is described as speaking "unto men for edification, exhortation, and consolation." Prophecy is the ministry of the Spirit building up the body. How is one exhorted, edified, or consoled? By the Word of God, which is the power of God for salvation (Rom. 1:16).

When Paul wrote his Corinthian epistle, the early believers didn't have the completed, written Word of God. Even the available *Septuagint,* the Greek Old Testament, cost so much it was beyond the reach of most Christians. But the early Christians enjoyed the ministry of prophecy and other charismata. Prophecy didn't replace the Bible, but it always agreed with it. That's why Paul said, "You can all prophesy . . . that all may learn and all may be exhorted" (1 Cor. 14:31). Learn what? The context demands that it must be either learning how to prophesy or learning from what is prophesied. Most Bible scholars agree: in this setting, prophecy is a form of teaching.

There are those who disagree, however. Susan Foh wrote: "First of all, prophesying must be distinguished from preaching . . . preaching is a form of teaching, and as such was forbidden to women in 1 Timothy 2:11-15. Prophecy is different in that God puts the very words into the mouth of the prophet."[1] Her argument is firmly founded on 1 Timothy 2:12 and if her understanding of this portion is incorrect, so is her conclusion. Dr. W.A. Criswell, pastor of the world's largest Southern Baptist Church, disagrees with her. "A preacher who gave forth the message of God in the wisdom and power of the Holy Spirit had the gift of prophecy. An inspired preacher was the first gift of the Spirit manifested in the church at Pentecost"[2] (cf. 1 Pet. 4:10-11, 1 Cor. 2:1-16).

Jesus commissioned the Church to evangelize the world. "Go therefore and make disciples of all the nations, baptizing them in the name of the Father and the Son and the Holy Spirit, *teaching* them to observe all that I commanded you; and lo, I am with you always, even to the end of the age"[emphasis mine] (Matt. 28:19, 20). Our Lord specifically told us to teach the nations, to herald the good news concerning the Son of God. Included in his directive are the ministries of evangelism, preaching, teaching, exhorting, witnessing and even electronic evangelism. Did Jesus forbid women from telling the good news? Were they restricted to prophecy?

Those who object to the idea that prophecy includes teaching fail to distinguish the *charismata* of prophecy from the office or *domata* of the prophet (1 Cor. 12:10; Eph. 4:11). All may prophesy, but not all are prophets. All may pray for the sick, but not all are anointed with the ministry of healing (1 Cor. 12:27). Furthermore, if 1 Timothy 2:11-15 forever excludes women from teaching when men are present as Ms. Foh asserts, then Priscilla, Phoebe, Jezebel and other women violated that principle.

When one prophesies, who is being addressed? "But one who prophesies speaks to men . . ." (1 Cor. 14:3). The word "men" is *anthropois,* meaning mankind in general, both men and women. Nowhere did Paul suggest that men's prophecy contained teaching while the women's did not. What were the words God put directly into the prophets' mouths as Ms. Foh asserted? Unless the spoken word in a Christian congregation contains truth for teaching, it shouldn't be uttered whether it's a song, a sermon or a Bible exposition.

"The basic difference between a prophetic utterance and the teaching message is the source. The prophetic word is a proclamation of a divine message. It signifies the speaking forth of the mind and counsel of God . . . forth-telling the will of God, whether with reference to the past, the present, or the future . . ."[3] A major portion of the Scriptures are written words of the prophets, who were moved upon and inspired by the Spirit of God. Teachers or explainers, however, don't speak from divine inspiration but from illumination as they make clear what has been spoken. Prophets are inspired, teachers are illuminated, but both are ministers anointed by the Holy Spirit. Why would the Spirit of God anoint women to prophesy but not teach? We know women were accepted as prophets in the early church. Jezebel, even though she was in error, was accepted by both the leaders and the church as a prophetess and teacher (Rev. 2:20). This weakens Ms. Foh's argument and arbitrary separation of the ministries of prophesying and teaching.

Anyone who prophesies, exhorts—providing teaching and guidance—and edifies and comforts, using the Word of God. This ministry is a charisma, a grace gift. If we harmonize Paul's statements in 1 Corinthians 11 and 14, we can honestly make this statement: Women may exhort, urge, advise, edify and comfort (all forms of teaching). Prophecy should be spoken publicly in the church where it can be judged (1 Cor. 14:29-31). If women can't prophesy in church where do they prophesy?

Paul said, "You can all [both men and women] prophesy one by one, so that all may learn [from what is being said under the anointing], and all may be exhorted" (1 Cor. 14:31). He gave absolutely no evidence, here or in his other writings, that this instruction is only for the men. Undoubtedly, the "all" includes both men and women.

Why prophesy? So that all may learn and be exhorted. "To learn," *manthano,* means to increase one's knowledge. To provide learning is the goal of teaching. "Exhort" is from the Greek *parakaleo,* meaning "to admonish, beseech, intreat or urge to some course of action," all verb forms of "teach." This doesn't negate the office of the teacher (Eph. 4:11), but neither does the office of the teacher nullify the validity of the individual believer prophesying and through his prophecy exhorting, edifying, teaching, admonishing and instructing so that all may learn!

Did Women Teach?

John recorded the book of Revelation after he was freed from the island of Patmos around A.D. 96. Any principle laid down by Paul in his Corinthian epistle would still be valid if it was a permanent injunction.

Christ Jesus admonished the church at Thyatira with some strong words: "I have this against you, that you tolerate the woman Jezebel, who calls herself a prophetess, and she teaches and leads My bond-servants astray" (Rev. 2:20). What an interesting statement! Jezebel both taught and prophesied, or she taught as a prophetess, and as previously stated, the leaders and elders of this New Testament church not only permitted her to teach, but accepted her and apparently believed what she said.

It stands to reason that if women were forbidden any type of teaching ministry and if women were silent in the churches, these Spirit-filled leaders would not have taken the time to listen to her at all. They had to give her permission to address the congregation. There isn't any evidence they were rebellious, ungodly or unspiritual. Her teaching must have been a normal occurence. If Jesus didn't want any woman to teach why didn't He rebuke her and establish a precedent? He could have said, "Women aren't allowed to teach in My Church! They must be silent and stop exercising leadership!" Surely He would have known that this sensitive issue would arise and would have given clear instructions to stop the practice. It would have solved this endless debate by spelling out once and for all exactly what he wanted.

Not only did this church accept her ministry, they heeded her teaching. Their action verifies that women prophet-teachers were not religious rarities. She functioned within an accepted ministry. If not, then this church was led by woefully immature, uninformed, and unspiritual leaders. Yet Jesus said He only had one thing against them. They allowed or encouraged (*apheis*) her as she led His servants into immorality and eating food offered to idols, actions prohibited by the first apostolic council (Acts 15:23-28). The Lord said nothing about her prophesying or teaching. He judged the content of her message and her ungodly actions.

Notice in verse 21 the Lord gave her time to repent of her immorality, not of her prophesying or teaching. Nor was Jezebel an isolated example. Phoebe was a "deacon" (Rom. 16:2) who was a "ruler" (*prostatis*) of many, including the apostle Paul. I used "deacon" since the feminine form, deaconess, wasn't used until at least 250 years after Paul wrote his letter. Prisca and Aquila were both teachers who worked with Paul (Rom. 16:3). So did Junia (a feminine name) and Andronicus, Paul's fellow apostles and prisoners (Rom. 16:7).

Did women teach? The only verse that says they can't is 1 Timothy 2:12, which directly contradicts Paul's other teaching, other biblical evidence, and the historical evidence. What can we conclude from our study? Did Paul silence the women? No! Who did? The same Judaizers whose oral law demanded the circumcision of all men, the veiling of women and the keeping of Moses' customs. However, Paul's teaching was based on Joel's prophecy: "In the last days . . . I will pour out my Spirit upon all flesh . . . and your daughters shall prophesy . . . and on my maidservants I will pour out my Spirit" (Acts 2:17-18 RSV). Paul knew that God chose women as well as men to speak His Word under the Old Covenant, and he knew that the Pentecostal experience fell on both men and women; they all prophesied and spoke in tongues. He knew that this manifestation included prophecy and that this gift proclaimed the Word of God as anointed exhortation, edification and comfort. He knew that this gift proclaimed the Word of God and predicted the future, and that women as well as men possessed this marvelous gift. So he told the Judaizers who wanted the women silenced, "And to you who keep on insisting that women be silent in the church . . . stop it!"

Chapter Five Notes

1.   Susan Foh, *Women and the Word of God* (Phillipsburg, NJ: Presbyterian and Reformed Publishing Co., 1979), p. 104.
2.   W.A. Criswell, *The Holy Spirit in Today's World* (Grand Rapids, MI: Zondervan, 1966), pp. 166-67.
3.   W.E. Vine, *An Expository Dictionary of New Testament Words,* (Old Tappan, NJ: Fleming H. Revell, 1966), pp. 221-22.

6

The Creation Order or Headship Before the Fall

"What can I do with my husband? He won't let me buy clothes for our baby. I can't do anything without his permission. I feel like a trapped slave. Is this God's will for me?"

When I counseled this young Christian mother further, she told me her husband had learned from his mother that he was the "boss" of his home, that it's the Bible way, since God created man first!

In a recent magazine interview, a well-known author said, "God commanded man to be the head, to have authority over the woman. It is important to realize that the headship of man is not an achievement, it is an assignment." I wrote a kindly letter asking this author how he arrived at this conclusion, but I never received an answer.

Assigned authority, submissive women, hierarchal headship and marital subjugation are assumed to be irrevocable and almost unquestionable Bible doctrines. However, if one is brave enough to question these dogmas, Genesis 2 and 3, the "order of creation" and "God's curse on woman" are almost always offered as proof. Nowhere in Scripture are there two other portions on which more interpretations or assumptions have been based than these two.

In answer to the question, "Why was there a need for male supremacy in Eden?" there's a standard two-part reply. One: God made man first, so he has priority. Eve was made as an afterthought as his "helpmeet," so her assigned position is one of submission to man's will and desires. The other part of the reply is Genesis 3:16: "Your desire shall be for your husband, And he shall rule over you." According to this interpretation, the two words "rule" and "desire" constitute man's assigned role as woman's overseer. Her desire shall be for man's company even though sorrow and submission are the result. Her relationship in marriage and to men is one of subjugation. Eve disobeyed her husband's authority; she sinned; therefore, she was forced into a permanent secondary role. These two passages constitute the basis for male supremacy.

The relevant Christian question is: "Did the apostle Paul promote a hierarchal order of authority: God-Christ-men-women-children? If he did, was it to amplify what God intended for men and women? Was an umbrella-like structure ordained by God at creation and reestablished at the Fall as a perpetual relationship? Is it a blessing or a curse?

Some teachers carry this idea into an ontological structure and claim women were actually created as serving creatures. John Calvin, a brilliant Reformation theologian, commented on 1 Timothy 2:12 by saying, "Women are by nature born to obey men." What he implied was, "Men are by nature born to govern and control women." Martin Luther expressed similar attitudes.

God's Purpose in Creation

The Church of Christ has a statement that fits well here. "Speak where the Bible speaks and be silent where it is silent!" Assumptions, long-standing traditions, private interpretations and accepted additions must be approached with extreme caution. Just what does the Bible say in Genesis 1 and 2 about the order of creation, and what is implied?

Hebrew tradition offers two opposing schools of thought about Eve's original status. One school of thought describes her as equal with Adam before the Fall, a co-regent, ruling with him as a fully equal partner. The other tradition portrays her as a subjugated inferior because she was created after him and became the cause of Adam's sin and death. The two opposing ideas are in stark contrast. Which one is right? What does the Word say? These two Jewish traditions are the same two accepted by the church.

As a Father, God yearned for a family created in His image and patterned after His Son (Rom. 8:29). His plan for them, outlined in Genesis 1:26-27, was to have them take complete control over His creation:

> And God created man [*Ha'adam*] in His own image . . . male and female He created *them*. And God blessed *them* and said to *them* . . . fill the earth, and subdue it; and rule [it] (emphasis added).

This was God's original statement concerning humanity. There's nothing in this verse suggesting man controlling woman or woman controlling man. They ruled together, equally sharing authority and dominion. The "law of first mention," a viable principle in understanding the Bible, says the first mention of a new truth establishes the context for it when spoken elsewhere. If we apply the "law of first mention" to the Bible, we must conclude that both of them were to rule the earth together. Nothing is said about the man having a position of authority over the woman.

Harmonizing Chapters One and Two

There are two different accounts of creation that still confuse some readers. Genesis 1 records the week of creation, climaxing with man's creation on the sixth day. Everything that happened during that eventful week led up to the grand finale, the creation of mankind. Genesis 2, however, has a different order of events. Man was made first (Gen. 2:7). Then God planted a garden in Eden and placed the newly formed man there (2:8). Verse 19 suggests that a period of time lapsed after man entered the garden, time enough for him to personally name all of the animals as God brought them before him. After all this, God then said, "It is not good for the man to be alone" (2:18). So He formed woman.

Which of these two accounts is correct? Chapter 1, which records the popular "week" of creation, or chapter 2, which has the detailed Adam and Eve account? In Genesis 1:26-27, male and female appear simultaneously as though created at the same time, while chapter 2 has at least some period of time separating their creation. Chapter 1 has man made on the sixth day at the end of the week, while chapter 2 has him created before the planting of the garden or the appearance of the animals.

Unfortunately, this seemingly confusing order has caused some to reject the creation account as primitive mythology. Other textual experts claim it was a collection of various accounts from at least five separate sources and compiled from them. However, according to a *Newsweek* article reported in *The Bible Newsletter,*[1] the theory that four sources, the "J-E-P-D" documents, form the basis for Genesis 1 and 2 has been refuted. Computer experts at Israel's Technion Institute fed the book of Genesis into a computer and found that it was probably written by one author, Moses. How can we explain the different accounts?

Genesis 1:26-27 is a simple declaration of God's purpose in

creating humanity both male and female. It has just the facts without the details. Chapter 2 tells us how He did it. The first account has both sexes appearing together while chapter 2 pictures God, like a potter working with clay, forming and molding first the man, later the woman. Genesis 1 gives us God's motive for creation; chapter 2 tells us how He worked it out. Chapter 1 doesn't tell us whether the male and female were created together or from what they were made. It only supplies the motive, the reason and purpose, nothing more. If the Spirit of God had left the account there we'd be left guessing about several important things.

Therefore, Genesis 2 introduces man, alone at the beginning of creation. Then God planted a garden as his home and gave him animals for companions. Finally, He formed woman from Adam's side. Actually, there isn't any conflict between the two accounts. According to *The Pulpit Commentary,* this is "in accordance with a well-known characteristic of Hebrew composition. The writer, having carried his subject forward to a convenient place of rest, now reverts to a point in time in the six days antecedent to man's appearance on earth."[2] In other words, Moses used a writing technique called "flashback." So we see there aren't two conflicting accounts but two parts of the same event and it's right here that most commentators become confused. If either chapter is neglected, the whole can't be understood and rightly interpreted. Chapter 2 must be read with and in the light of the revelation of chapter 1.

Chapter Six Notes

1. Nov. 1981.
2. Vol. 1, p. 43.

7

Male and Female Made He Them

When God said, "Let us make man," was He referring to just the man Adam or to all humanity? This is important since God said "man" would rule His creation. If the first physical man, Adam, is meant, it stands to reason that Eve, made later, would be part of the creation he would rule.

God's command was given to *them,* not *him. God's original statement must govern our thinking on this subject! Ha'adam,* with the definite article *ha,* used in Genesis 1:26, 27 for "man," is not the proper name Adam with an article. *Ha'adam* is a generic term meaning "humanity" or "mankind." That's why the plural "them" is used. If God meant a single person, the pronoun "I," "he," or "him" would have been used, but not "them." This text tells us God did not give His command to rule just to one person, but to all humanity, including the soon-to-be-made woman.

This difficult passage troubled the ancient rabbis. Although they spoke Hebrew as a native tongue, in their pre-conceptions they believed woman was the source and cause of sin; therefore, her subjugation had to be God's punishment. The "them" troubled them as did the "us" and "we" when God said,

"Let *us* make man in *our* image." How could God address "them" when there was only one, the man Adam? Some rabbis said Adam was bisexual. Others said he was both male and female within one body with all the functions and possibilities of both male and female. We know from Philo's writings that this theory was still tossed about during the days of Christ: Adam's inner man was male, his outer man was female, his spirit was male but his soul was female; when God formed woman He separated the female soul from Adam and put it into her own body. This was a confusing proposition since it left Adam without a soul and Eve without a spirit.

"He created them male and female, and blessed them and named them Man [*ha'adam*] in the day when they were created" (Gen. 5:2). *Ha'adam,* with the definite article, isn't used after Genesis 5:2. After this reference the article is dropped and the word *adam* becomes the proper name of the man, Adam. Understanding the simple usage of this word, without the mystical interpretations of the rabbis, the mystery of Genesis 5:2 vanishes. God specifically called both man and woman *adam.*

Genesis doesn't use the word "create" for the origin of Adam, the man, but a different word, "formed." See how it is used in Isaiah 44:2, 24 and 49:5 without the sense of a specific creation. Then turn to Isaiah 43:1, 7 or 45:18 where it definitely refers to a progressive development. Israel was formed and developed but never created. This is the same word used in the Genesis 2 account and the same idea expressed by Paul in 1 Timothy 2:13 where he said, "Adam was first formed [or developed], then Eve" (KJV). Genesis 5:1-2 says both male and female were created, not developed. In God's mind, both Adam and Eve were created simultaneously; however, Adam was formed first, and Eve was formed later to complete the creation of man (*ha'adam*). There isn't any contradiction between the two accounts. Neither was Adam created a sexual freak with both male and female characteristics. Nor is there any clear evidence that God assigned man the position of ruling the woman as her head by forming him first.

Woman Made a Helpmeet

Doesn't helpmeet or helpmate mean she was created for man's sake, to be his helper under his authority? Wasn't she made specifically for man? ". . . man is the head of a woman . . ." (1 Cor. 11:3). "For it was Adam who was first created, and then Eve" (1 Tim. 2:13).

It's true God "fashioned" woman from man's side (Gen. 2:22), but this doesn't make her a lesser person to be subjugated. We must ask a simple but relevant question: Why did God make woman?

The original idea for woman's creation comes from God, not Adam. He didn't ask God for her. Actually, after he willfully sinned and God challenged him, he as much as said, "It's the woman's fault. If you had not given her to me it wouldn't have happened!" It was the Creator's idea to make woman. "It is not good for the man to be alone." Man's "aloneness' was more than just being alone as a person. Linguists tell us the expression "one alone" as in Joshua 22:20 or Isaiah 51:2 is a different Hebrew form. The expression in Genesis 2:18 means, "in his separation." Was Eve brought forth to help Adam recover himself as some theologians suggest? Was there some weakness in the primal man that needed woman? The Scriptures are silent so any answer is pure conjecture. But we know for sure the idea of woman's creation was God's and not Adam's.

God said, "It is not good for the man to be alone: I will make a helper suitable for him" (Gen. 2:18). As soon as man saw her he said, "This is now bone of my bones, And flesh of my flesh; she shall be called Woman [*Ishah*], Because she was taken out of Man [*Ish*]." To be fully happy and complete, mankind needs relationships and communication between equals. As humans we can enjoy animals; they can afford some companionship, but they are not communicators. God foreknew Adam's need for oneness with an equal companion, but Adam needed to recognize that need himself. Genesis 2 reveals how God made that need known.

First, He formed the animals and birds, and Adam named them, a process which must have taken some time. Meanwhile, Adam must have noticed the original pairs multiplying as a result of their togetherness. Of all the creatures passing before him, not one was a suitable companion for him (Gen. 2:20). Gradually, he realized his aloneness; he was incomplete and helpless. Then God said, "I will make him a helper suitable for [or corresponding to] him"—someone capable of meeting his needs.

"Meet" is an old English word meaning, "fit," "proper," or "suitable." It has the idea of joining, combining, union, or togetherness without any sense of division. Since she was taken directly from man's side, she is all he is, nothing more, but nothing less.

The Mythology of the Rib

The idea that woman was made from man's rib is more fictional than factual. I heard a minister preach, "Man has one less rib than woman because man's rib was used to form woman." Of course this isn't true and such irresponsible statements hinder the spreading of the gospel. Both men and women have the same number of ribs.

In *God's Word to Women,* Dr. Bushnell quoted the *Englishman's Hebrew Concordance* and *Young's Analytical Concordance* and other sources saying:

> The Hebrew word *tsela,* "rib" is a mistranslation.
> Forty-one times it is translated "side," "corner,"
> "chambers," or "flank."

She also gave the origin of the rabbinical mythology of the rib.

> One story says that "Eve was made out of a tail
> which originally belonged to Adam." Rav, the head
> of the Babylonian rabbinical school declared, "Eve
> was formed from a second face, which originally
> belonged to Adam." Another rabbi said, "Instead of
> a rib taken from Adam, a slave was given to him to
> wait upon him." But the originator of the "rib"
> theory was Rabbi Joshua, who wrote, "God
> deliberated from what member He would create
> woman, and He reasoned within Himself thus: I
> must not create her from Adam's head, for she
> would be a proud person, and hold her head high. If
> I create her from the eye, then she will wish to pry
> into all things; if from an ear, then she will wish to
> hear all things; if from the mouth she will talk much;
> if from the heart, she will envy people; if from the
> hand, she will desire to make all things; if from the
> feet, she will be a gadabout. Therefore, I will create
> her from the member which is hid, that is, the rib,
> which is not even seen when man is naked."[1]

The Bible says God made her from man's side, but Jewish
fables said she was made from his rib.

It's amazing how theologians take one simple verse and
work it over until any semblance of the original truth is gone.
But that's the story of religious confusion, each theorist telling
the world what God really meant since He couldn't, wouldn't
or didn't say what He meant and didn't mean what He said.
Why did Rabbi Joshua subsitute the word "rib" for "side"
knowing it was an incorrect translation? Apparently to
strengthen the low opinion most rabbis had of women, to
justify masculine insecurities built upon the false premise that
woman and not man was responsible for sin and death.

Does Helper Mean Server?

'Ezer kenegdo is the Hebrew translated as "helpmeet" or "helper." John Calvin said it means "inferior aid."[2] Others, such as Abel Isakesson, said it means "to bear his children." Keil and Delitzcsh, commenting on this passage, said, "Of such a help the man stood in need, in order that he might fulfill his calling and perpetuate and multiply his race."[3] These men forgot that God gave the command to fulfill to *ha'adam*, both male and female; it wasn't his calling but "theirs." Most rabbis still agree with Isakesson even though a gradual change is taking place in Orthodoxy today. They consider woman to be foremost a sexual creature and as such belonging entirely to her husband, created to bear his children.

Susan Foh wrote, "The woman was created to help the man . . . The woman was created to be a help to her husband; her function is dependent on him. He makes the decisions and she follows."[4] If this statement is correct, women were created to marry. Without a husband to make her decisions, a woman would be like a fish without water. Without a husband to depend on and help she would have no real purpose in life. If women were created just to help and obey, created for their husbands, then without a husband a woman would be out of God's will. Yet Ms. Foh conceded that Paul's God-given advice is that it's best for the unmarried women not to marry (1 Cor. 7:1-25). She admitted that "the end of marriages means the end of the woman's subordination to her husband."[5] If a woman doesn't marry, the subordination of woman to man is nullified.

Is it true the priority and authoritative position of man hinges on the rib theory of creation? Is there something hidden in the word "helpmeet" we've overlooked, or has tradition added something we've accepted that has drastically changed what God meant when He said He would give man a helper?

Did He say, "I'll make him a helper to serve him"? Or did He say, "I'll make him a co-worker, a co-regent who is exactly like him, who will fulfill, sustain, satisfy and work with him and he with her. She'll be his associate, not his assistant!" Is there anything in the word "helper" that says she is one who assists and not an equal associate?

'Ezer kenegdo describes a stronger party supporting one in need. Foh wrote, "Perhaps in reaction to this low opinion of women, many modern theologians try to find connotations of superior help in the Hebrew word *ezer* (helper)."[6] She quoted scriptural references but then ignored them and continued her thesis that woman was made to help her husband. She correctly stated that *'ezer kenegdo* doesn't imply inferiority or superiority but equality. "More importantly, the helper of man is *kenegdo,* that is, corresponding to or like him, neither inferior or superior." This is double talk! There may not be inferiority of persons but there certainly is inferiority of position; therefore, the two are not on an equal footing. For example: Army privates are equal to their superior officers in that they are human beings, but who doubts they are definitely inferior in position, acceptability, capability and authority? Foh's idea that man came first and woman must be his helper is pure interpretive assumption even though she quoted 1 Corinthians 11:9. She should have read verse twelve where Paul balanced this proposition. Yet she insisted there isn't any sense of inferiority between the sexes, even though the ancient rabbis said woman was inferior, even though the primitive societies treated her as inferior, even though she was created as a serving creature.

> The woman is created to be a help to her husband; her function is dependent on him. The temporal priority of the man is significant. The woman followed his lead in the creation process, and she is to follow his lead as her husband.

> This sort of reasoning may not be convincing;
> it obviously has not convinced many Christian
> women. It has been said there was a 50-50 partner-
> ship between the husband and wife, and that the
> headship is a consequence of the curse . . .
> However, the order of creation is significant
> according to the New Testament (1 Cor. 11:8-9;
> 1 Tim. 2:13).[7]

She admitted her argument isn't convincing! Many Bible students see Paul's balance in 1 Corinthians 11:11-12 where he said that God is the originator of both sexes, and that since the first birth, man has no longer preceded woman, because he now has his beginning in woman.

Instead of binding the female to a life of submission to men and marriage, why not loose her with this possible interpretation?

God made woman, not for man to rule, control, or make decisions for, but to be an equal partner who would rule with him and care for the garden with him. Who gave the orders? Who made the decisions? God! (Gen. 1: 26, 28; 2:15). Sin had not yet corrupted mankind. Strife, aggressiveness, domineering attitudes, and the struggle for preeminence were unknown. Mankind bore the image and likeness of God himself. They acted like God, talked like God, loved like God, interacted like God, cared for one another like God, and accepted each other as God accepted them. In that they loved like God, Paul said in 1 Corinthians 13:5: "love does not seek its own." Where there's the God-kind of love, there isn't any desire to take charge of another person. Whenever I hear "Who was in charge?" I hear the voice of sinful man striving for dominance.

Genesis 2:18 is void of any aspect of man's authority over woman. The immediate context is reproduction and not masculine preeminence! Had God created woman first He would have created man for the same reason: neither can reproduce alone.

After God said "It isn't good for man to be alone," He created the animal kingdom, but none of them was suitable for man's needs. That's when God "built" a helper for him. The context isn't hierarchal but biological. It wasn't a question of woman "helping" Adam rule the earth but of "filling the earth." The "helper" helped man fill the earth, and, during my lifetime, mothers always have had preeminence in the birth process.

Paul used this thought in 1 Corinthians 11:12 to correct the very overbalance we've been discussing. "For as the woman originates from the man [the supposed basis for man's delegated authority over woman], so also the man has his birth through the woman [this cancels his primal position]; and all things originate from God." "However, in the Lord, neither is woman independent of man, nor is man independent of woman" (v. 11) is the key. Without this revelation, verse 3 (man as the head of woman) and verse 9 (the woman was created for the man's sake) remain unbalanced. Paul knew all too well the injustice Judaism used to repress its women and he sought to correct the error. It was the blight of sin that brought submission, authority, rulership and oppression into the world. A curse, to be sure, but who wants to help fulfill a curse?

Ms. Foh quoted Clarence Vos as saying, "The other Old Testament references to *'ezer;* 15 times it refers to God as the helper, and 3 times, to the help of man, which is ineffectual . . . Thus if one excluded Genesis 2:18, 20 it could be said that ONLY GOD gives effectual help (*'ezer*) to man."[8]

When David said, "My help comes from the Lord," he used the same word. The same word is used in Psalms 30:30; 115:10; 146:56; Exodus 18:4; Deuteronomy 33:7, 26, 29. Fifteen times it means "superior strength" and it's the word God used for Eve. It certainly can't mean physical strength since we know females are physically weaker than males, although that is relative. Someone once said, "If God left childbearing to the men that would have been the end of the race!" Nevertheless, Peter exhorted the men to dwell with their wives as with a weaker vessel so their prayers wouldn't be hindered (1 Pet. 3:7). The only logical conclusion is woman must have either mental or spiritual strength.

Kenegdo means the front parts, opposite each other, or answering to each other. When combined with *'ezer* it means equal parts, alongside.[9] *The Pulpit Commentary* states, "She was to be of similar nature to the man himself, corresponding by way of supplement to the incompleteness of his lonely being, and in every way adapted to be his co-partner and companion."[10] Or as Dr. Judson Cornwall said, "She was his alter-ego, once facing him exactly like him."

This sounds similar to a precious New Testament revelation about our Lord Jesus. "He is the radiance of His glory and the exact representation of His nature" (Heb. 1:3). Even as Jesus was God's glory, so woman was man's glory. One without the other is incomplete. Jesus came to make God known to mankind, to manifest His glory (John 17:5). Likewise, without woman, man would have been incomplete, helpless, incapable and unable to change the situation. Thank God for His marvelous wisdom.

God Gave Man an Associate

We must be careful not to overstate our case, but one fact is obvious: woman wasn't created just as man's assistant or server. She was to be an associate, a co-worker with full rights and privileges. She was added strength to fill his weaknesses. Ms. Foh listed several valid reasons why God made woman from man's side rather than as a separate creation.[11]

- It is part of her corresponding to him.
- God's creative act is one act beginning with man and ending with woman.

- All humanity comes from one source, Adam. Because he is the source—"as in Adam all die"—he represents all humanity.
- Woman's creation sets up the principle of one flesh in marriage.
- Even though woman was made second, from and for the man, she isn't his inferior but his equal.

Had she stopped there, no one would disagree with her. But she added her interpretation: "The man's priority in creation corresponds to headship over his wife." This is an implication read into the account. I'm sure Adam knew nothing of this principle or else he would have submitted to the animals who were created before him. If "the first is the leader" is a principle, does it always apply?

Woman wasn't a luxury or an afterthought, but a vital part of God's original plan outlined in Genesis 1:26, 27. That's why Genesis 2 must be balanced by Genesis 1 or we'll end up following the ancient rabbis in their fanciful interpretations. Without both male and female there would have been no procreation, emotional fulfullment, social welfare or spiritual development.

The reason God didn't make Eve a separate creation is implicit in the creation account. God said she would be someone exactly like man or corresponding to him. If she were a separate creation made from dust as man was, she couldn't be a part of his flesh and bones. This makes a major difference between humans and animals. Actually, woman was the finished aspect of God's initial creation. The fact that she was made some time after her male counterpart doesn't mean she was made to be his servant, handmaid or assistant.

During a series on "Family Feuding," John MacArthur said, "God provided this suitable helper to aid Adam as he ruled the pure and undefiled world of creation. Notice from the very beginning, God designed someone to be in charge, and someone to help; someone to be in authority; and someone to be submissive; someone to be the leader, and someone to be the follower." Yet he said earlier when dealing with the "curse" in Genesis 3:16, "So as part of this curse God says to the woman, 'You were once co-regents, wonderfully ruling together as a team, but from now on the man is installed over you.' This was a new kind of ruling—an authority never known before."[12]

On the one hand he said that the man and woman worked as a co-equal team before the Fall just as God said (Gen. 1:26, 27), and that male supremacy came about as a result of Eve's sin, a new kind of ruling authority they had not known before the Fall. In other words, Dr. MacArthur said, man and woman worked together as equals until sin disrupted the harmony.

Yet he taught there was an authority-submission posture before the Fall even though it wasn't visible: "From the very beginning the man had the role of headship, and the woman had the role of the one for whom the headship was provided." Foh said her reasoning isn't very convincing and MacArthur said the headship wasn't visible. The teaching of feminine submission and masculine authority and headship aren't found in Genesis before the fall except where an interpreter forces them into the context. Without these assumptions, there isn't anything in Genesis 2:18 that says the woman was created to serve her husband, as the rabbis taught.

It seems more in keeping with the scriptural revelation we have of God's impartial nature that God would give man a fellow co-worker, a co-regent to rule with him, an associate with full rights and privileges, also made in the likeness and image of God. The man and woman supplemented and fulfilled each others' needs. God gave the commands and made the decisions, and together Adam and Eve fulfilled them.

Let's let Matthew Henry, the Puritan commentator, bring this chapter to a close. "Man being the last of the creatures, as the best and most excellent of all, puts an honour upon that sex, as the glory of man (1 Cor. 11:7). If a man is the head, she is the crown; a crown for her husband, the crown of visible creation. The man was dust refined, but the woman was dust double-refined, she was one step further removed from the earth." Thank you, Matthew Henry, that's nice!

Chapter Seven Notes

1. Katherine Bushnell, *God's Word to Women* (1923; privately reprinted by Ray Munson, N. Collins, NY), pp. 39, 42, 43.
2. *Commentaries,* Vol. 1, p. 69.
3. *Commentary on the Old Testament,* Vol. 1, pp. 86-89.
4. Susan Foh, *Women and the Word of God* (Phillipsburg, NJ: Presbyterian and Reformed Publishing Co., 1979), pp. 61, 215.
5. Ibid., p. 180.
6. Ibid., p. 60.
7. Ibid., pp. 60-61.
8. Ibid., p. 60.
9. E.A. Speiser, *The Anchor Bible* (Garden City, NY: Doubleday, 1964), p. 17.
10. Spence & Exell, *The Pulpit Commentary, Vol. 1* (Grand Rapids, MI: Eerdman's, 1950), p. 50.
11. Susan Foh, *op. cit.,* p. 61.
12. John MacArthur, *Family Feuding and How to End It* (Panorama City, CA: Word of Grace Communications, 1981).

8

Is There a Superior Sex?

In November 1982, *Reader's Digest* published an article, "Is There A Superior Sex?" which raised a number of questions and answered some. For each male strength there is a weakness that finds it strength in the female. For example: men aren't as immune to disease as women. Females tend to be gifted in verbal skills while most males are not. On the intellectual scale, males have more retarded members as well as more geniuses. Men have heart disease at an alarming rate compared to women, and the argument that women entering the work force will suffer the same fate as men is as yet without evidence. Actually, working women have better health than home-makers.

Men are more skilled in mathematics, and environmental differences don't alter the fact. Men are better at abstract thinking. They also work better with their hands than women.

More males than females are born dead. Males die younger and fewer reach maturity. Most violent crimes are committed by males. Alcoholism, hyperactivity and schizophrenia are primarily male problems, while more females suffer depression. This enlightening article verified what God already said, that man needs woman and woman needs man to be complete. The male's weaknesses are the female's strengths. The two make one person. Because men are aggressive, domineering and want to take charge doesn't mean God made women to be servants.

Some writers such as Scanzoni and Hardesty, Christian authors of *All We're Meant To Be,* and Goldberg, author of *Inevitability of Patriarchy,* suggest hormones make the difference, and scientific studies seem to support their conclusions. Rats fed increased levels of testosterone increased their hostility and aggressiveness; but then, rats are not humans.

According to Scanzoni and Hardesty, the mentally healthy male is aggressive, independent, unemotional, logical, direct, adventurous, self-confident and ambitious while the mentally healthy female is passive, emotional, dependent, less competitive, nonobjective, submissive, vain, easily influenced, religious and insecure. The male traits are called adult or mature while the female traits are called childish or neurotic.[1]

Sociologists are aware that social orders are based on generations of fear, prejudice and ignorance with the scales weighted in favor of the male. The *Tulsa World,* on December 5, 1982, carried a feature: "Labels, Assumptions Diminish Women." It showed the bias reflected in our language. Men are termed aggressive, women pushy. Men get annoyed, women hysterical. Single fathers are praiseworthy, single mothers are not. Men assess their lives, women have empty-nest syndrome. Men are ambitious, women clawing. Man's stress is job-related, woman's is due to nerves. An overworked man is a go-getter, an overworked woman disorganized. Men are versatile, women flighty. Older men look distinguished, older women dowdy. The double standard and prejudice are obvious.

Margaret Mead's work among primitive tribes raised some questions about the hormonal explanation of differences in behavior. In one tribe she studied, the women were dominant, unadorned and authoritative while the males were dependent, gossipy, and vain about their appearance. Her work pointed out the role society plays in determining personal behavior.[2] I must disagree with Rev. Larry Christenson's statement, "The heart of woman is more easily discouraged and dejected. God made her that way."[3]

If anything, most wives keep discouraged husbands afloat. Discouragement, rejection, fear, and insecurity are sins of the flesh, the result of unbelief. How could God create discouragement and weakness in a perfect human being and call it good? The two weaknesses he blames on God are both the consequences of sin and unbelief. Where there is active faith there isn't any discouragement or rejection since "Faith is the assurance of things hoped for, the conviction of things not seen" (Heb. 11:1). Christenson's fellow Lutherans disagree with him. In 1972 The American Lutheran Church published a brief dealing with the sexes in the church and society which stated: "Qualities such as gentleness, compassion, helpfulness, and artistic appreciation are found in varying degrees in both males and females as are qualities of assertiveness, vigor, initiative and strength. All human beings are created in God's image, and the mystery of femaleness and maleness is to be celebrated as one of God's gifts."[4] Why do we classify qualities as gentleness, compassion, and helpfulness as feminine qualities when Paul said they are the fruit of the Holy Spirit? (Gal. 5:22). These aren't feminine qualities but an expression of the nature of God himself. It isn't hormones that make bullishness, but sin. It isn't femaleness that makes one gentle or longsuffering, but the Spirit of God. In other words, male and female are equal as persons, in position, and in possibilities of success, except where tradition, bias, ignorance or prejudice hinders them. They are complementary in their sexuality and mutually related in their wholeness. They need one another to be complete.

Chapter Eight Notes

1. Letha Scanzoni & Nancy Hardesty, *All We're Meant To Be* (Waco, TX: Word Books, 1974), p. 73.
2. Susan Foh, *Women and the Word of God* (Phillipsburg, NY: Presbyterian and Reformed Publishing Co., 1979), p. 167.
3. Larry Christenson, *The Christian Family* (Minneapolis, MN: Bethany Fellowship, 1974), p. 128.
4. Margaret Howe, *Women and Church Leadership* (Grand Rapids, MI: Zondervan, 1982). p. 149.

9

Oneness as God Is One

And God said, "They shall become one flesh" (Gen. 2:24). When Adam woke and saw his "helper" he said, "She shall be called Woman ['ishah—Hebrew feminine] Because she was taken out of Man [ish—Hebrew masculine]." Grammarians tell us the masculine 'ish, meaning "man," has the feminine suffix ah added to it. 'Ishah, "woman," is taken from 'ish, "man," the only difference being the feminine suffix. One writer made an interesting comparison: "'Ishah was taken from 'ish, the same way ha'adam was taken from ha'adamah, the ground." If woman must submit because the man was made first, one can see the problems involved. If woman was made to submit to man because she was taken from him, then man should submit to the ground from which he was taken.

They Shall Become One Flesh

And the man said, "This is now bone of my bones,
And flesh of my flesh; She shall be called Woman,
Because she was taken out of Man" (Gen. 2:23).

The Living Bible has a cute paraphrase here. "When Adam saw his wife he said, 'That's it!'" He knew why she was there and rejoiced. Dr. John MacArthur stated it nicely: "They were co-regents. They ruled together. The headship and authority-submission isn't even visible because prior to sin, it was so beautiful, so God-created, so God-ordained, so pure, and so pristine that they multiplied together, filled the earth together, subdued the earth together, and ruled together."[1] What he said is beautiful, but untrue. The first child wasn't born until *after* they sinned and were banished from Eden (Gen. 4:1), so they did not multiply together, fill the earth, etc. But what he said about authority-submission not being visible in the Scriptures is enlightening. If it isn't visible, how do we know it existed except by our editorializing and interpreting what we think might have been involved?

The commanding Adam and the obedient Eve aren't visible. The authoritative man and the submissive woman aren't visible. The striving man taking charge of the resisting, rebellious woman isn't visible. The frustrated woman withstanding man's bullish aggressiveness isn't visible *until after sin and death gained control of mankind.* Before the Fall, none of this was visible nor does anything in the Scriptures say it was there. The only area of submission involving Adam and Eve was God's command not to eat of the tree of the knowledge of good and evil. Why was anyone needed to make decisions for another to obey? God gave them *both* (*ha'adam*) the command to care for the garden.

The statement "They shall become one flesh" has a two-fold meaning. Primarily it means the physical oneness necessary for procreation, but Paul gave it a deeper meaning. In Ephesians 5:31 he compared the spiritual union of Christ and the Church to the natural union of the husband and wife. Since there isn't a physical union between the resurrected Christ and the Church, it has a deeper spiritual meaning.

"They shall become one (*'echad*) flesh." To grasp the meaning of *'echad,* see how it's used in Deuteronomy 6:4, a passage quoted daily by all orthodox Jews. "Hear, O Israel! The Lord is our God, the Lord is one [*echad*]!"

'Echad generally means a compound unity rather than a single entity. It takes more than one thing to make an *'echad*, a united togetherness. The word for single or solitary is *yahid*. Alone, Adam was *yahid*, Eve was *yahid*, but God joined them together as an *'echad*. The two became "one" just as the Trinity is one. Within the Godhead, the Father, the Son, and the Holy Spirit are one. In the Scriptures, *yahid* isn't used as frequently as *'echad*, and *'echad* is sometimes used for a single thing; however, since Paul used Genesis 2:24 to illustrate the union of Christ and the Church, this "oneness" takes on a special significance.

Jesus prayed that the Church would be one just as He and the Father are one in the Trinity (John 17:22, 23). The Church's failure to be one with her head is the basic reason the world doesn't believe Jesus is Lord after two millenniums of worldwide witnessing. Paul used the body simile to teach the unity of the body members and the unity of the body with the head (1 Cor. 12).

Is There a Trinitarian Hierarchy?

Some capable Bible teachers say yes! Others say no! If God made woman to submit to man's assigned authority, there must be a similar hierarchy within the Godhead because Paul used this comparison in 1 Corinthians 11:3. God is Christ's head just as Christ is man's head just as man is a woman's head. Unless there is a parallel this statement is irrelevant. Notice also that man is head of "a woman." Not all women, just as "a woman," leading most scholars to single out wives.

Paul Jewett wrote in *Man as Male and Female,* "God is a fellowship in himself so Man is a fellowship in himself, and the fundamental form of this fellowship as far as man is concerned, is that of male and female."[2] Jewett mentioned that Karl Barth, the German theologian, promoted the same idea, writing: "Man in the image of God is Man as male and female."[3] Foh rejected this analogy because there is little scriptural support for it. She did say the relationships—God as Christ's head and the man as a woman's head—illumine each other.[4] But this forces another question: "Can there be a hierarchal arrangement among absolute equals?" Foh said yes, but in the real world it isn't so!

A hierarchal relationship within the Trinity implies three separate persons, co-equal and co-eternal, with the Father taking the position of authority, the Son the position of submission and the Holy Spirit submitting to both the Father and Son. Foh listed several Scriptures to prove her point:

"I and the Father are one" (John 10:30).

"I can do nothing on my own authority; as I hear, I judge; and my judgment is just, because I seek not my own will, but the will of him who sent me" (John 5:30).

"The Father is greater than I" (John 14:28).

Then Foh added, "Christ is fully God (John 1:1; Col. 1:15-20), and yet God is his head (1 Cor. 11:3; 15:27-28)."[5] In her reasoning, submission and equality somehow complement one another.

Before His incarnation, the Logos was God the Creator (Cor. 1:16). He existed from eternity. Before Him no God was formed and none after Him (Isa. 43:10). He was the first and the last, and there is no God besides Him (Isa. 44:6; c.f. Isa. 44:24; 45:5-7; 45:22, 23). Nowhere do the Old Testament Scriptures suggest there was anyone greater than the Lord himself.

Since His ascension, Jesus has a name greater than any name in heaven, on the earth or beneath the earth (Phil. 2:9-10). His throne is above every throne. Angels worship Him! There is none greater than He! There is abundant scriptural proof that the pre-existent Logos was God (John 1:1; Phil. 2:6-7). There is evidence that the now-reigning Christ is King of kings and Lord of lords (Phil. 2:9-11). When was Jesus in a position to say "the Father is greater than I"? During His earthly existence.

In *A Systematic Theology of the Christian Religion,* Buswell wrote: "In the recorded words of Jesus, the divine Sonship designates a relationship of absolutely essential equality. . . . all reference to the subordination of the Son to the Father signify a *functional subordination* in the economy of the divine redemptive program. It is of the utmost importance that we distinguish between *economic,* or *functional subordination,* and *essential equality.* When Jesus said, 'The Father is greater than I' (John 14:28), and 'I can of my own self do nothing' (John 5:30), we must understand these statements as referring to His economic subordination in 'the days of his flesh.'

"But when he said, 'The Father does not judge anyone, but he has given all judgment to the Son, in order that all should honor the Son even as they honor the Father. He who does not honor the Son does not honor the Father who sent him' (John 5:22, 23); 'I and my Father are one' (John 10:30); it should be clear that in these passages we have to do with the essential relationship of equality."[6]

Paul exhorted the Philippian church to voluntarily submit to one another, esteeming others better than themselves. Then he used Christ as an example of humility. Christ, who was the Word and with God (John 1:1), humbled himself and took the form of a servant and was obedient unto death. He laid aside His equality!

"Who existing [and continuing to exist—Greek tense] in the form of God, thought it nothing to be attained to [or grasped or held on to] to be equal with God, but emptied Himself taking the form of a slave and was made in the likeness of men."[7] What He relinquished was not His Godness—as Deity He could never be less than Deity—but the independent exercise of His will and divine attributes.

What He laid aside was His privilege of free choice. His knowledge was limited; his power was dependent on God; He was in the form and position of a slave. As such He was limited and learned obedience by the things He suffered. Why learn obedience if He had always been obedient? He did not consider His equality with God (*He was God*) something to be clung to. As the Last Adam He obeyed God even as the First Adam disobeyed God.

When Jesus ministered in the name of the Lord, He said the works He did were the works of His Father in heaven. Anyone honoring Him honors the Father; anyone knowing Him knows the Father; anyone rejecting Him rejects the Father. He emphasized and demonstrated His total equality with Deity, giving the Jews grounds for demanding His death. What did He do? He did the works of God by speaking the Word of God. If honoring, knowing, or rejecting Jesus is equal to honoring, knowing, or rejecting the Father, then Jesus is equal to the Father.

Scriptures such as John 14:28 suggesting a hierarchy within the Trinity are limited *only* to the time of His humiliation on earth. During His earthly ministry Jesus willingly took a position of obedience but only because He had become the Last Adam. As a perfect sacrifice and substitute He had to voluntarily lay aside His equality and will for absolute submission.

But that dispensational subordination was completed at the ascension. The glory He shared with the Father before the world began was restored (John 17:5). Everything He willingly laid aside as man's redeemer was restored (Phil. 2:10, 11). The original oneness, the *'echad* within the Godhead, was restored. Never again would He have to be humiliated. He was given a name above any name in heaven, on the earth or below the earth. At the mention of His name, hell quivers, demons shudder, Satan stutters, and heaven worships. He is both Lord and Christ, Yahweh and Messiah! Subordinated? Never again!

And something marvelous took place because of His resurrection. He conquered Satan and his demon hordes once and for all (1 John 3:8; Col. 2:15). The original oneness man and woman shared was restored! The curse of sin was removed. All the struggle of headship, taking charge, bossiness, rebellion and the like was removed because they are sin! Christ opened up a new and living way. Man can once again enjoy the oneness God promised.

Genesis 1 and 2 record God blessing man with a source of extra strength to counterbalance his weakness, and blessing the woman with strength to counterbalance hers. Together, a husband and wife make one whole person just as God in Trinity is one. This is the reason Paul used the example of marriage to explain the mystery of the Church and Christ. Even as the Church is His body, He has highly exalted her and seated her with Him in the heavenly places (Eph. 2:6). Not as an assistant or helper but as an heir of God and joint heir with Christ. All dominion, authority and power in heaven and earth belong to the Church and are at her disposal (Eph. 1:17-23). Whatever she binds on earth is being bound in heaven. Whatever she looses on earth is being loosed in heaven (Matt. 16:19; 18:18). But He can do nothing unless we ask or tell Him what to do. "If you ask Me anything in My name, I will do it" (John 14:14). The "if" qualifies the promise. If you don't ask, He can't do anything.

Rather than asking us to obey Him, He has limited himself to doing only what we pray, ask or demand. I realize the implication of these categorical promises but we aren't destined to be servants forever; we are destined to reign with Him.

Is there as Trinitarian hierarchy? There was, but only during the days of our Lord's earthly ministry when He willingly laid aside His glory, equality and authority to take man's place and redeem him. That time of servanthood, of humiliation—when Deity was made flesh, when He suffered by learning obedience, when the Father was greater in position than He, when He was man—is completed. Once again He is King of all kings, Lord of all lords, possessing a name greater than any name in heaven or elsewhere. Nothing and no one is greater than He!

Chapter Nine Notes

1. John MacArthur, *Family Feuding and How to End It* (Panorama City, CA: Word of Grace Communications, 1981), p. 33.
2. Paul Jewett, *Man as Male and Female* (Grand Rapids, MI: Eerdmans, 1975), p. 14.
3. Ibid., p. 35.
4. Susan Foh, *Women and the Word of God* (Phillipsburg, NJ: Presbyterian and Reformed Publishing Co., 1979), p. 58.
5. Ibid., pp. 99-100.
6. James Buswell, *A Systematic Theology of the Christian Religion* (Grand Rapids, MI: Zondervan), p. 106.
7. Ibid., p. 703.

10

Who Caused Sin and Death?

> Yet your desire shall be for your husband, And he
> shall rule over you (Gen. 3:16).

This verse is the second one allegedly making woman's submission and man's domination a divine decree. Because Eve believed the serpent's lie and then tempted her husband to sin with her, supposedly usurping Adam's authority by acting on her own, God punished both her and her female descendants for all time. One teacher said, "Because woman refused to submit to her husband's authority before the Fall, she was now ordained by God into that role." If this assumption is true then women should accept their fate and submit to male domination, regardless of the meanness of men.

Eve's transgression caused at least three changes in her life. Her conception was greatly multipled, her motherhood was bathed in sorrow and heartache, and she was now ruled by her husband. Because this last statement is so distasteful to a Spirit-filled Christian, especially in the light of generation after generation of wife abuse, it is sometimes softened to say, "Even though man is woman's head, he should not rule her as common chattle, but love her with Christian love." However, it rarely works out that way in actual practice. Muslims, Jews, pagans, primitive societies and many hyper-fundamentalists control their wives and households with a stern hand.

Does this verse say God cursed women? Were women punished with a curse that even the blood of Christ can't or hasn't yet removed? More basically, was Eve responsible for ushering sin and death into the world and with it sickness, poverty, demonic control, and everything that is wicked and evil? Did Eve tempt Adam into sinning with her? Has she been cursed with a sexual desire bordering on disease as one Talmudic writer said?

We've learned how ancient Judaism taught that Eve caused Adam's death and destroyed his life, light and glory. Many Evangelicals agree with that. *Eternity* magazine in December 1980 published an article, "Paul, Women and the Church," which compared the writings of fifteen authors who dealt with Paul's five key passages on the woman question. Their diversified answers illustrate the confusion still surrounding the issue. Few of them agreed on everything but their answers reveal a "follow the leader" mentality since they quoted each other as their sources of information. However, one theme emerged through this maze of religious thinking, authored by liberals and conservatives, men and women: Men have the dominant role in life by virtue of God's judgment on Eve's sin. One writer said women were created for the role of submission. Another said women glorify God by fulfilling men's desires. Several agreed that the order of creation applied to Christian practices. Three women writers concurred that women were subjected by divine decree. Perhaps they sought to maintain their denominational status quo. We know that many "sacred" traditions are simply falsehoods that have been around so long they have been accepted as truth. We must be careful we don't become modern fulfillers of our Lord's warning: "Full well ye reject the commandment of God, that ye may keep your own tradition" (Mark 7:9 KJV).

Did Eve Tempt Adam?

This question is foundational since the liberty of at least half the Church depends on the conclusion. When God placed "the man" in the garden He told him to dress and guard it against all intruders. This is implied since the word "guard" (AMP) means to protect or watch over. There was only one restriction hampering his absolute freedom. "From any tree of the garden you may eat freely, but from the tree of the knowledge of good and evil you shall not eat" (Gen. 2:16-17).

The only reason for this one restriction was to test their wills. God made mankind with the freedom of choice, a free will, and let them decide whether or not they would obey. Evidently God did not want spiritual zombies who functioned like mechanical robots; He wanted a family of children made in His image and likeness who would love and work with Him. They were fully capable of making decisions and choosing right and wrong. Although God gave this command to Adam personally some time before He formed the woman, it included all humanity (*ha'adam*). Adam must have told Eve what God had said since she quoted it to the serpent during the temptation (Gen. 3:2-3).

God told the man he was to guard and keep the garden. Did Satan, using the serpent, approach Eve because Adam was more experienced? Was she tempted because she was the weaker vessel? Was she usurping Adam's authority by acting on her own? Was Eve doing in a very careless manner what Adam should have been doing, guarding the garden?

Where Was Adam During the Temptation?

Why didn't Adam warn his wife and help her overcome temptation if he was in charge? The late Dr. M.R. Dehahn told a tender love story about Adam during this temptation.

"Adam was away fellowshipping with God when this tragedy took place. As soon as he realized what had happened, his deep love for Eve forced him to lovingly, willingly, voluntarily forsake his intimacy with God and join himself to his now sinful wife as a token of his great, sacrificial love." Dehahn called it "The Greatest Romance Known," basing the story on Romans 5:14 and used it to illustrate the love of Christ leaving the fellowship of God and becoming one with fallen, sinful humanity in order to redeem us. It's a beautiful, touching scene but it isn't scriptural. *Was Adam separated from his wife when this crisis happened?*

He was not! He stood by her side during the whole sorry episode. When Satan spoke to the woman, he didn't speak to her alone. He said, "You [you and Adam, both of you] surely shall not die" (Gen. 3:4). This is implied because Eve handed the fruit to "her husband with her" (Gen. 3:6). When Eve picked the fruit, did he make any effort to stop her? When she handed it to him he accepted it. Notice Genesis 3:7: "Then the eyes of both of them were opened," again implying it happened to both of them at the same time. If Adam had any primal authority there isn't any evidence he used it. I repeat what Dr. John MacArthur said, "It isn't visible."

Paul debunked the idea that Eve tempted Adam. He said Adam was not deceived or tempted either by Eve or the serpent (1 Tim. 2:14). That's why Paul said Adam sinned in a way no other human has ever sinned (Rom. 5:14). The temptation made the difference. Eve sinned because she was thoroughly deceived. Adam sinned as a rebel in a treasonous act against God.

Stating that Eve gave her husband the fruit later means ignoring that he was "with her." The idea that Satan attacked Eve as the weaker vessel, knowing she would drag her husband along after her, is pure speculation and completely illogical. If she was weaker, why would Satan expect her to seduce her husband to sin with her? Apparently Adam willingly let his companion be deceived. Eve did not usurp Adam's authority. If the primal right of authority was his, this was the only recorded opportunity for him to use it, and he failed. He was a passive partner. Surely something as tragic as this, since it deals with the female half of society, would have been recorded by the Spirit in detail. But all the scriptural record tells us is Adam was not deceived, Eve was! Therefore, Adam was the clear-headed one who could have stopped the affair. All he had to say was, "Satan! Get out of my garden, and Eve, don't let me ever catch you talking with a snake again!" But he didn't! Who was responsible for sin? The Bible says Adam was!

Whose Sin Was Worse?

Sin, regardless of its name or color, is still sin. Nevertheless, Paul said that Eve was thoroughly deceived, but that Adam was not (1 Tim. 2:14). Her deception wasn't just a passing thing like someone promising to fast and then sneaking a doughnut. She was completely convinced that her actions were all right. Deception is more than breaking a law even though you know the consequences; it's believing the thing you're doing is actually right. For example, there are cultists who will gladly die for their faith although we know they are wrong. The 900 followers of Rev. Jim Jones in South America were deceived, even to the point of committing suicide with their faces on the ground. Call it mind control; it's still deception. Many Jehovah's Witnesses have spent part of their lives in prison because of a deceptive concept about participating in military affairs. We believe they're wrong, but they believe they're right and they are willing to spend time in jail to prove it. When Eve offered the fruit to her husband she was thoroughly deceived, she thought it was the right course of action.

The word "deceived" in both of these New Testament passages has a prefix which means "thoroughly." Weymouth translated it "the woman was thoroughly deceived and so became involved." However, when Paul said Adam wasn't deceived he used what is called an emphatic negative which means "absolutely not." This should settle the question of whether Eve tempted Adam to sin with her. Paul said, "Absolutely not!"

Who Caused Sin?

> Through one man sin entered into the world (Rom. 5:12).
>
> By the transgression of the one the many died (Rom. 5:15).
>
> By the transgression of the one, death regained through the one (Rom. 5:17).

More than eight times Paul said "one person" caused the Fall, and twice he named that person as Adam. That's why Christ is called the Last Adam and not the Last Eve, clearly implicating the first man as the cause of sin and death.

Although both man and woman sinned, God held the man responsible, not because he had the primal right of authority over the woman, but because he was a deliberate rebel. Purposely, and without any evidence of temptation, deception, persuasion or coercion, he turned from God to sin and Satan. He took a calculated risk and lost, knowing full well what could happen. His act of treason was as willful as that of Lucifer, the archangel, who sinned and became the enemy of God.

Paul wrote in 2 Corinthians 11:3 that Satan gained control of Eve's mind by using his skilled craftiness. He appealed to her physical senses. He challenged her natural reasoning powers and her senses took over. We can imagine her thoughts: "The tree *looks* good for food. It *feels* nice and it smells divine. After all, God said it was the tree of knowledge of good and evil and would make us wise. We would be better equipped to serve the Lord." What happened was this: Satan worked on her mind, her imagination, and her intellect through her senses. The knowledge the tree would give them was appealing.

Her mistake was letting Satan force her faith into the arena of reason. The moment they tasted the fruit, they became self-conscious and aware of their nakedness. They lost the conscious presence of God. They fell from righteousness into the quagmire of sin-consciousness. They were dead to God! It would be many years before their physical bodies stopped functioning, but at that moment they were dead to God's presence. They were completely separated from Him and committed to a material world, no longer led by God's Spirit but by their five senses, their minds, and their emotions. Death, the wage of sin and the punishment warned of by God, entered their lives.

The wage of sin is still death regardless of the magnitude of sin. The only difference between their separate actions was that the man acted without any outside influence, temptation, provocation or coercion. Neither Eve or Satan tempted him or talked him into disobeying God's command; he acted solely on his own initiative. That's why sin entered the world through the man and not the woman.

Chapter Ten Notes

1. John MacArthur, *Family Feuding and How to End It* (Panorama City, CA: Word of Grace Communications, 1981), p. 33.

11

Did God Curse Eve?

The degrading power of the tree of knowledge began its work. Fearfully sulking and burdened with sickening guilt, the man and woman did the only thing that seemed reasonable. They tried appeasing God, hoping to soften His anger. Although they knew nothing about death, nor had they ever seen anything die, they had a foreboding fear. Apparently, they assumed that covering their nakedness would help the shame and guilt go away. In so doing they established man's first efforts to justify himself before God by means of good works. And thus came to be, from within man's fallen nature, the seedbed of all religion. A satirist might call it "The First Holiness Church of the Fig Leaf." When they rejected God's word, they substituted what they thought was right and reasonable, the fruit of the tree of knowledge of good and evil. God found them neatly dressed in their miniskirts.

"Who told you you were naked? Have you eaten from the tree . . .?" God asked.

"The woman whom Thou gavest to be with me, she gave me from the tree and I ate" (Gen. 3:12). What he really said was, "God, it's really your fault! You gave her to be with me. I didn't ask for her, it was your idea. If she wasn't here I probably wouldn't have eaten the fruit!"

Turning to Eve, Yahweh said, "What is this you have done?" As God He knew what they had done. His interrogation was for their confession. Satan watched anxiously as she implicated him. "The serpent deceived me, and I ate" (Gen. 3:13). Her answer was forthright and honest; she didn't blame God or Adam. Nor did she sidestep her responsibility. She accepted the blame; she confessed the source of her problem. She didn't do a Flip Wilson and say, "The devil made me do it!" She accepted her part in the tragedy.

Let's compare the two replies. Both admitted eating the fruit—how could they deny it? But Adam actually blamed God for giving him the woman. In effect he said, "You made me do it!" Indirectly he shielded the serpent, an act of treason. Eve's candid confession placed her back on God's side but spiritually separated her from her husband. Paul's revelation in 1 Timothy 2:14 tells us Adam wasn't deceived. Eve's sin was a result of deception; Adam's was deliberate rebellion.

The Curse

First, God cursed the serpent as the vehicle Satan used. "Cursed are you more than all cattle, And more than every beast of the field" (Gen. 3:14). Tradition tells us that prior to God's cursing the serpent it was a beautiful creature that held Eve's admiration with its ability to communicate vocally. Now it had been degraded to the lowest of animals, a crawling creature eating dust. "On your belly shall you go!"

The effects of the "curse of sin" touched all creation since death affected both men and animals, but the serpent was cursed over and above the penalty of death. Yet in a strange way, the serpent became a type of Christ, who would become sin and take the "curse" upon himself (2 Cor. 5:21; Rev. 21:5-9).

Turning to Adam, God said, "Cursed is the ground because of you." From that moment thorns and thistles, weeds and seeds, insects and diseases have plagued every growing thing. That's why Paul wrote in Romans 8:20-23, "Creation itself will also be set free from its slavery to corruption . . . creation groans . . . waiting eagerly for . . . redemption."

Continuing, the Lord said, "In toil you shall eat of it All the days of your life. By the sweat of your face You shall eat bread, Till you return to the ground" (Gen. 3:17-19). Unfortunately, man has tried to repudiate this statement. He can't reverse it so he does everything possible to avoid it. In many countries I've seen pregnant women with babies strapped to their aching backs working the soil in their husband's place. There are still societies where men marry as many as four wives and put them to work doing what God said was man's chore.

Did God Curse Man and Woman?

It's important we speak where the Bible speaks and be silent where it is silent. *Nowhere does it say God cursed either the man or the woman!* It does say He cursed the serpent and the ground because of man, but that's all! Anything more than this is assumption or forcing an interpretation on the Scriptures. Nor is the curse of the man or woman implied anywhere else in the Scriptures. Why? Because God had already told them exactly what would happen if they ate from the tree . . . they would die! The wage of sin is death! The curse of sin is death!

God didn't curse them; He told them what the consequences of their sin would be. Man "would," not "must," work by the sweat of his brow since his food would come from the now cursed earth. It wasn't a special sentence laid on him but the result of his actions. *Adam's curse was death, not sweat!* Nor did God curse the woman! He told her, just as He told Adam, what the consequences of her sin would be.

Then He made a covenant with her that through her seed (not man's) a deliverer would someday come and reverse the disastrous events that had just taken place. The "seed" would bruise the serpent's head and destroy his hold on humanity (Gen. 3:15).

Second, her pain and sorrow in childbearing would be greatly multiplied (Gen. 3:16 KJV). This is the verse the rabbis used to prove the wife's sex life must be controlled by the husband's personal choice, and the reason Paul challenged the Judaizers in 1 Corinthians 7:4 by saying the body of the husband belongs to the wife even as the body of the wife belongs to the husband.

Misinterpretation of this verse has added fear and pain to childbirth, which is actually a natural event ordained by God. God did not condemn women to painful pregnancies nor did He make sex unlawful, unspiritual or dirty!

The Hebrew word *itstsabown* means "sorrows" or "trial" and it is translated this way in the Septuagint, the Greek version used by the early Christians. Even though there are those who still believe God punished woman with painful pregnancies, no early believer would have received that idea from their Bible. *Itstsabown* is translated as "toil" in Genesis 3:17 where it describes man's sweaty efforts to make the earth produce. The same word should be translated in Genesis 3:16 as "I will greatly multiply your toil."

Bushnell, in her book *God's Word to Women,* wrote "the word here, [the Hebrew word for conception] in its original vowel-less state fails *by two letters to spell conception.*"[1] Without these two letters the word means "sighing" or "groaning," the word the Jewish translators used in the Septuagint. Their choice was an excellent commentary since they were masters of their traditions and language. They did not use the word "conception" in Genesis 3:16. Her groanings, toil, and sorrows were greatly multiplied. Can anyone deny that Eve had great sorrow and heartache when she discovered her firstborn son had brutally murdered his younger brother? That's the fruit of sin.

Logically, the idea of "cursing" Eve with painful conception is difficult to grasp since conception hadn't taken place yet. It would be painful compared to what? How or why would God increase something that was still unknown?

"Yet your desire shall be for your husband, And he shall rule over you" (Gen. 3:16). Unfortunately most reference Bibles give a single reference for this verse: 1 Corinthians 14:34-35, leaving the impression that this verse somehow justifies the silencing of women and making her public utterances shameful. It's important, then, that we try to unravel this statement since more than one half of the church is involved: the women.

Turning Desire Into Lust

The word *teshuqa* ("desire") only occurs three times in Scripture: Genesis 3:16 and 4:7, and Song of Solomon 7:10. Most dictionaries say it means "to stretch out after," or "to long for," which closely parallel our English word. Dr. MacArthur, a well-respected scholar, said the word comes from an Arabic root which means "to compel, to impel, to urge, to seek control." After comparing the word in Genesis 3:16 with 4:7, where there is little doubt as to its meaning, he stated, "therefore, 3:16 would rightly read: 'To the woman He said, . . . your desire will be to control your husband, but he will rule over you.' " He continued, "Historically, women have never loved their role of submission to their husbands. There isn't a period in history where women weren't chafing underneath male authority."[2]

Does *teshuqa* have sexual overtones as the rabbis indicate in their writings? If so, when was this meaning first used? We've already learned the ancient rabbis believed that God cursed Eve and her descendants with ten curses, based on the assumption that woman brought sin into the world.[3] Although Paul gave us God's truth on the matter in his Roman epistle, a number of contemporary scholars seem to agree with the rabbis. "She was punished with a desire bordering upon disease," wrote Keil and Delitzsch in their *Commentary on the Old Testament.*[4]

"Thou shalt desire nothing but what thy husband wishes," wrote John Calvin. Calvin also implied God ordained marriage but later substituted servitude.

"It is part of her punishment, and a part from which even God's mercy will not exempt her. Subjection to the will of her husband is one part of her curse," wrote Adam Clarke. In most areas Clarke's scholarship is excellent but his personal prejudices reveal his human weaknesses and the reason no one should ever completely rely on the commentaries of men. Apparently, according to Clarke, the blood of Jesus left part of the alleged curse intact. Does *teshuqa* mean "desire," "lust," or "servitude"?

Ben Sira, one of Israel's most influental rabbis, wrote *The Wisdom of Ben Sira,* also known as *Sirach* or *Ecclesiasticus.* He was the first to suggest that woman caused sin. "From woman a beginning of sin, and because of her all die" (Sir. 25:24). His strong influence on other rabbis who followed him can't be denied since the Talmud contains no less than four of his opinions and statements. He wrote during the early years of formative Judaism in the second century B.C.

His ideas helped warp the thinking of many early Christian fathers. Irenaeus, Bishop of Lyons in 177, took up Ben Sira's unscriptural comments by adding, "Having become disobedient she became the cause of death, both to herself and to the entire human race." Tertullian, another Church Father, blamed Eve for sin: "Do you know that you are an Eve? You are the avenue to the forbidden tree . . . you persuaded him [Adam] whom the devil himself had not the strength to assail . . . You are the first who deserted the divine law. For your desert—that is, death—even the Son of God had to die."[5] Ambrosiaster wrote, "The man is created in the image of God, but not the woman. Because sin began with her, she must wear this sign [the veil]."[6] To these and other Church Fathers, "desire" meant sexual longing.

Can we honestly say that this "desire" is a strong sexual longing for her husband or that it's her "desire" for the man to rule her? Pragmatically speaking, men have a much stronger sexual desire than do women. It's this stronger "desire" that keeps many marriages in turmoil, so this interpretation is out. Nor can we realistically conclude that women desire to be ruled by men.

What Is the True Meaning of Teshuqa?

Dr. Bushnell shed some interesting though unorthodox light on the word *teshuqa*. The stem is derived from the verb *shug,* meaning "to run." All Hebrew words are built on a stem, with a prefix, suffix or medial added, giving the stem a full range of meanings. The prefix *te* gives the word an abstract sense, and it corresponds to our termination, "-ness" in such words as "goodness" or "kindness." The ending *a* is added to give a word the feminine form usual in Hebrew abstract nouns. If this word were taken from the intensive form of the verb, it would bear the sense of "to run repeatedly," that is, "to run back and forth." But to keep running back and forth would necessitate frequent turning. The sense "desire" has come to us from the Talmud, in the "Ten Curses of Eve." Dr. Bushnell said Eve was "frequently turning" toward her husband, so Bushnell rendered Genesis 3:16: "You are continually turning toward your husband, and he will rule you."

Then she listed six very ancient versions which also use "turning." The older Babylonian Targum, now a part of the Talmud, uses "turning" rather than "desire." We do know the

Septuagint translates *teshuqa* with the Greek *apostrophe* in Genesis 3:16 and 4:7, and with *epistrophe* in Song of Solomon 7:10-12. *Thayer's Greek Lexicon* gives these meanings for *apostrophe:* "to turn away, to attempt defection, to turn away from allegiance, turn back, return." Bushnell said, "Eve is turning away from God to her husband, and, as a consequence of that defection, Adam will rule over her."[7] John MacArthur gave this meaning: "Your desire will be to control your husband, but he will rule over you."[8] My preference is: "Even though men and marriage will be painful and filled with sorrow, even though your husband will rule you, you'll still desire his company, but *he will rule you!*"

He Will Rule You

The Hebrew *yimshal,* derived from the verb *mashal,* means "to rule" or "to have dominion." Here's the core of God's statement.

Was God commanding Adam to rule his wife? Was He putting Eve in her proper place and telling her to submit? Is it true that she usurped Adam's authority and ended up sinning? That God established her subjugation to the man once and for all? Did God, in this one statement, assign Eve and all women to a life of submission? And did God *add* to His original judgment ("in the day that thou eatest thereof thou shalt surely die")? Was He now adding subjugation as additional punishment for her sin? Not if the Hebrew sentence construction means anything!

If God ordered such a command, the verb "shall" or "will" would have been in the imperative mood—a command. But according to scholars, this verb is in the simple imperfect, and not a command at all. The verb form in the simple imperfect translates into English as the future tense. In other words, the statement is prophetic in that God told Eve what would happen as a consequence of her sin. The imperative is only found in the present tense, so this simple imperfect tense prevents translation of "shall" as a command. It doesn't say man *"shall"* but *"will"* rule her; it's not a command but a consequence. God did not tell Eve she *must* bear children, but that she *would.* He didn't tell Adam "you *must"* work by the sweat of your brow, but "you *will."* He didn't say that men *must* rule and dominate women, but that they *will!*

What the Lord really told Eve can be paraphrased: "Eve, because you have sinned, and because Adam sinned, circumstances have changed. You'll have a normal desire to be with him; you'll keep turning toward him, but he'll rule you. He doesn't have my nature any longer; he now has the nature of the devil. He's a tyrant now! Instead of loving, he now hates. No longer is he patient and gentle, but totally selfish. His former kindness is gone; he's now brutal and self-centered. He's a rebel and a sinner and as such he'll dominate and rule you. Your grief and sorrow will be greatly multiplied. Heartache and pain will follow you all the days of your life. I don't want it this way, but because of the terrible thing the two of you have done, that's the way it is. This isn't the curse I warned you about—the curse of sin is death, but this is a warning of what will be. You've brought this upon yourself; it's the consequence of sin. But there is hope. I give you my Word, the Promised Seed will come and reverse this tragedy. The enemy who deceived you will be totally crushed and your former position as an heir of God will be restored; but until that day comes, trust Me!"

From the Fall of man, women have been oppressed, opposed, dominated, cruelly ruled, and subjugated to man's selfish gain. If the Hebrew verb in Genesis 3:16 were in the imperative mood and a command from God rather than a warning, then the more forcefully a man domineered a woman, the more completely he would fulfill the letter of the law.

If Genesis 3:16 were a curse on all women, it would work against the whole tenure of the Scriptures. If rabbinicism were correct and this passage demanded the subjugation of women, what did Christ accomplish at the cross? Did He die for Adam's sin but not Eve's? Did all the old things pass away and all things become new (2 Cor. 5:17) except the subjugation of women? Or did the all-powerful blood of Jesus avail for all sin except Eve's?

Man's authority over woman, whether taught by the rabbis or the Church Fathers, isn't God's will or law. Paul's instructions to slaves regarding submission to their owners didn't make slavery right. It was a social issue, an accepted "wrong" of that period, and it has long been rejected as completely unchristian and immoral.

This, then, is the biblical background for woman's debasement and man's exaltation, woman's submission and man's dominance. Even though it was a man who brought sin and death into the world, it is women who have suffered the most. Doesn't it seem strange, if not contradictory, that man should be exalted to the position of lording it over woman when he was the guilty one? However, that is exactly what God said would happen. Not because the Almighty decreed it, but because fallen man would sinfully enforce it!

Conclusion for Chapters 10 and 11

God stated His divine purpose in Genesis 1:26-27: humanity, both male and female, would be made in His image and both would rule together under His authority and fill the earth. There isn't any evidence one was designated to rule and the other to submit, one to lead and the other to follow, one to take care of the provisions and one to be provided for. This is a religious interpretation and assumption, the ground on which denominational differences are built. Before the Fall there wasn't anyone from whom to protect the woman, nothing to provide for her; they lived in Paradise where God watched over both of them and provided for them.

There isn't any evidence that because Adam was made first, the second on the scene automatically served him as his helper. If this principle were valid then mankind, created the day after the animals were made, should have served them. Woman was given to man as his associate, his co-worker, his co-regent, a source of extra strength to fill in his weaknesses. Without her he was incomplete, and without him she would have been incomplete. Together they made one whole person.

Both sinned, but Adam refused to accept the responsibility for his actions, so he was judged as the one bringing sin and death into the world. The serpent and the ground were cursed but not man or woman. God had already told them if they ate of the tree, the punishment would be death, not sweat for Adam or submission for Eve. As a direct fruit of their sin the ground would resist their efforts to produce their food, while women would be ruled by sinful men determined to dominate everything. History has yet to record a time when women have willingly accepted this role of submission even though Christian women *try* to accept it. Most chafe. Nor has this consequence of sin been a blessing even though some counselors say it can be. It's the result of ungodly men and women warring with one another in the sin-filled state.

Finally, God promised a Redeemer, a Virgin-born Seed, one who would crush the serpent's head and restore humanity to a relationship with God (Eph. 2:5). Quite frankly, as a Christian husband I have no desire to dominate or rule my wife. She's my best friend, and friendship can't exist where one always gives in to the other. Gladys and I have a partnership, no, a trinity, where Christ is the third person and absolute Lord, and together we are co-regents.

Chapter Eleven Notes

1. Katherine Bushnell, *God's Word to Women* (1923; privately reprinted by Ray Munson, N. Collins, NY), pp. 120, 121ff.

2. John MacArthur, *Family Feuding and How to End It* (Panorama City, CA: Word of Grace Communications, 1981), pp. 34-35.

3. *Babylonian Talmud,* Erubin, 100b.

4. C.F. Keil and F. Delitzsch, *Commentary on the Old Testament* (Grand Rapids, MI: Baker Book house, 1977).

5. *The Fathers of the Church, Vol. 40,* trans. Arbesmann, Daly & Qualin (New York: Fathers of the Church, 1959), p. 117ff.

6. *Patrologia Latina, Vol. 17* (New York: Adlers Foreign Books, 1857), col 253.

7. Katherine Bushnell, op. cit., p. 131.

8. John MacArthur, op. cit., p. 35.

12

Headship in Paul's Epistles

Most women are comfortable with Jesus' attitude toward them since none of His words or deeds suggested inequality between the sexes, even though He ministered during the close of the Old Covenant and the heyday of the oral law. But Paul's writings sometimes intimidate women with his seemingly contradictory statements about women's place in the home and church.

Was Paul Confused About Women?

Some of his teaching was revolutionary. The New Covenant canceled the old order, which had been a shadow of better things to come. Beginning with the crucifixion of Christ there was neither Jew nor Greek, male nor female, bond nor freeman; Christ was all in all (Gal. 3:28; 2 Cor. 5:17). In the Kingdom of God there is no hierarchy, no second-class citizenship. Each person is a unique, redeemed individual, a joint heir with Christ regardless of sex, nationality or position in society. The beginning of the Kingdom marked the end of superior-inferior, lord-servant, priest-peon, Jew-Gentile status. However, centuries of traditions aren't easily changed.

Look at slavery! For generations sincere Christians promoted it and used the Bible to defend their practice. After the Civil War, the Ku Klux Klan began a quasi-religious organization spitting venom and hatred in the name of Jesus. History records the Crusades, the torture chambers of the Inquisition, and the heresy trials, all practiced in the name of the Lord, but what genuine Christian today would approve of these dark-age horrors? Nevertheless, they existed and they died hard. Even though Paul's revelation of our utter oneness in Christ set both men and women free, others believe he reimposed the ancient rabbinical customs on the church.

Paul made four statements (1 Cor. 11:3; Eph. 5:22-24; 1 Tim. 2:11-12 and Tit. 2:3-5) which form the framework for advocating a hierarchal order: God-Christ-man-woman. What was Paul proving?

Context and Background

The New Covenant began with Christ's death and resurrection, marking the end of the old and the beginning of the new (Gal. 4:4; Eph. 1:10). The divine breakthrough of Christ established His Kingdom for ever. The salvation foreseen by the ancient prophets had clearly come (Acts 3:19-25; 2 Cor. 6:2), and the dawn of the New Creation had arrived. Everything Adam's sin brought upon the human family was canceled.

Believers were now free from the law (Rom. 6:14) and the curse of the law (Gal. 3:13). They were free from demonic control and power (Col. 2:15), free from the works of Satan (1 John 3:8), and free from all condemnation (Rom. 8:1). They were living in the Kingdom of God (Col. 1:13). Going back to Adam, every demand had been met and fulfilled. Everything evil brought into the world by Adam's sin, including woman's subjugation, had been removed by the Last Adam. And wonder of wonders, man's desire to aggressively dominate was replaced by the love of Christ which is described, "Love doesn't seek its own" (1 Cor. 13:5).

We've seen the powerful influence Judaism had on the infant church. Most of the earlier converts were Jews who for the most part wanted to enjoy their new-found freedom without letting go of their Mosaic customs. To them, Judaism was more than a religion; it was a lifestyle, a badge of identification. Even though they had accepted Jesus as their Messiah they didn't forsake their traditions. Naturally, they wanted the new Gentile converts to live as they lived, since Christianity wasn't considered a separate sect but a part of Judaism. You can understand why Paul's New Covenant theology troubled them. But these zealous Jews weren't the only problem. There were the Gnostics, so called after the word *ginosko,* which means "to know."

The Gnostics claimed a supernatural knowledge beyond any human understanding. They taught a dualistic view of the world that exalted the spirit while debasing the flesh. The material world as described by them was controlled by demons and was inherently evil. Only the spirit world mattered to them. As a result they divided man into two separate beings: the divine spirit, and the evil flesh. When baptized into Christ, they considered the spirit set free from the body of flesh, free to soar unaffected by the world.

Some of them believed they had already been made perfect through Christ's resurrection (1 Cor. 4:6-8). Their error was failing to see the difference between the legal and experiential aspect of redemptive truth. Because they considered themselves already perfected they claimed a special knowledge, supposedly received through estatic visions and tongues. Whatever they taught was supposed to be pure truth since it was of the spirit. The results were disastrous.

Some of the Corinthian Gnostics renounced marriage while others defrauded one another by living together without sexual contacat. Others were libertarians, indulging in gross immoralities since they considered flesh and spirit to be separated. One man lived with his own father's wife (1 Cor. 5:1).

They also had a theology of androgyny which said the perfected spirit was neither male nor female since these fleshly distinctions belonged to the evil world. Their super-spiritual other-worldliness blotted out such distinctions. That's why Paul corrected them by saying that even though we are new creatures, this doesn't blot out the existing social structures. Marriages must remain intact. Jews shouldn't efface their circumcision any more than Gentiles should get circumcised. Slaves were to maintain their position for the present. Christ didn't come to destroy society but to impregnate it with eternal life through obedience and repentance. Believers are in the world but not of the world. This was the social and historical context in which he addressed the matter of headship.

The Difference Between Head and Heart

How did the Christians reading Paul's epistles understand the term "head" or "headship"? How is it used in the Greek New Testament? *Kephale* is used 57 times, and 50 times it refers to the physical head of a man or animal. But Paul used it figuratively seven times, and these are the particular passages we'll study. Of the seven times *kephale* is used figuratively, only two of them are interpreted as meaning male-dominant headship (1 Cor. 11:3 and Eph. 5:23) so we'll give them special attention.

The commonly accepted meaning is one of authority or superior position, but the meaning isn't that clear-cut in the New Testament.

F.H. Palmer's *New Bible Dictionary,* under the title "Head," says, "The head is *not* [italics mine] regarded as the seat of the intellect but as the source of life . . . Thus to lift the head is to grant life in the sense of success (Judges 8:28)."

Harper's Bible Dictionary says, ". . . the heart was metaphorically regarded as the source of man's intellectual activities."[1]

Wilson's Dictionary of Bible Types says, "The word heart is used in the Scripture to indicate many attitudes of the mind and many various kinds of affections and reactions."[2]

The heart, the inner man, was thought to include his intellect, will and emotions. Almost all authorities agree that the heart was considered the source of thought and emotions and the "head" the source of life. Note the psalmist's cry, "Though an host should encamp against me, my heart shall not fear. . . . When thou saidst, Seek ye my face; my heart said unto thee, Thy face, O Lord, will I seek" (Ps. 27:3, 8 KJV). But the heart doesn't speak or think, the mind does. To say, "Thy blood be upon thy head" was to charge a person with responsibility for life and death. (cf. Josh. 2:19, 1 Kings 2:37). When the high priest laid his hands on the head of the scapegoat, he symbolically laid the collective sins of Israel on it. The animal's head represented the source of life, substituting for the life of the people. To them, the head was the source of life.

Even Plato, a pagan philosopher, said man's soul was in his heart, the seat of intelligence and emotion. As scientific knowledge increased, men discovered the heart wasn't the seat of intellect, the mind was, and the head wasn't the source of life, the heart was. Therefore, if we force a modern understanding, even though it's more accurate, into the ancient usage of *kephale,* Paul's true meaning is lost.

God's laws weren't written on man's mind but on his heart (Ps. 37:31). Man's heart doesn't think, his mind does; but to them it was just the opposite. The springs of life proceed out of the heart (Prov. 4:23). We read, "As he thinketh in his heart, so is he" (Prov. 23:7 KJV). However, we now know the heart pumps blood and has nothing to do with thought processes. Paul said we must believe in the heart in order to be saved (Rom. 10:9). Yet the context was preaching and hearing the gospel, information received through the head.

When Paul used *kephale*—"head"—he meant what we think of as the heart.

Chapter Twelve Notes

1. Madeleine and J. Lane Miller, *Harper's Bible Dictionary,* (New York: Harper & Row, 1973).
2. Walter L. Wilson, *Wilson's Dictionary of Bible Types* (Grand Rapids, MI: Eerdman's 1957).

13

The Head of the Epistles*

What did the apostle Paul mean when he wrote, "For the husband is the head of the wife as Christ is the head of the church, his body" (Eph. 5:23)? And, "The head of every man is Christ, and the head of the woman is man, and the head of Christ is God" (1 Cor. 11:3)?

Discussion about the biblical role for men in church, society, and home is based on these verses. The meaning of these verses rests largely on the meaning of the Greek word *kephale,* translated "head" in the New Testament.

One possible way the word "head" is used today means leader, chief, or director. We say, "He is the head of his company," or, "He is the department head." In husband-wife and male-female relations this idea popularly carries over to suggestions of authority. The husband is said to be the boss of the family. Before we accept that idea, we must ask what the Greek word *kephale* (head) meant to Paul and his readers.

---

*   This chapter was written by Berkeley and Alvera Mickelsen, professors at Bethel Theological Seminary in St. Paul, MN. It originally appeared as an article in *Christianity Today,* Feb. 20, 1981, and is used by permission. All Scripture quotations are from the Revised Standard Version, unless otherwise indicated.

To find the answer, we must first ask whether "head" in ancient Greek normally meant "superior to" or "one having authority." In the first half of this article we will introduce three kinds of evidence:

1. Lexicographers Liddel, Scott, Jones, and McKenzie *(A Greek-English Lexicon,* ninth edition, Clarendon Press, 1940, a really comprehensive Greek lexicon) gives no evidence of such a meaning.

2. The Septuagint translators took pains to use different words than "head" *(kephale)* when the Hebrew word for head implied "superior to" or "authority over."

3. In his commonly used lexicon *(A Greek-English Lexicon of the New Testament and Early Christian Literature,* William Arndt and F. Wilbur Gingrich, eds., U. of Chicago Press, 1957/1979), Walter Bauer gives little or no salient support for such meaning outside of his personal interpretation of five Pauline passages in the New Testament.

In the second half of the article, we will answer the fundamental question: If "head" does not normally mean "superior to" or "authority over," what does it mean in those seven New Testament passages where Paul uses it figuratively?

First, what about the differences in the lexicons? One of the most complete Greek lexicons (covering Homeric, classic, and *koine* Greek) is the work by Liddell, Scott, Jones, and McKenzie. It is based on examination of thousands of Greek writings from the period of Homer (about 1000 B.C.) to about A.D. 600, which, of course, includes New Testament times. Significantly, for our purposes here, it does not include "final authority," "superior rank," or anything similar as meanings of *kephale.* Apparently ordinary readers of Greek literature would not think of such meanings when they read "head."

However, another commonly used lexicon is the *koine* Greek lexicon by Arndt and Gingrich (usually called Bauer's). It does list "superior rank" as a possible meaning for *kephale.*

It lists five passages in the New Testament where the compiler thinks *kephale* has this meaning. As support for this meaning in New Testament times, the lexicon lists two passages from the Greek translation of the Old Testament, the Septuagint, where *kephale* implies leadership or authority.

Those who support Bauer's view that *kephale* meant "superior rank" point to these passages in the Greek translation of the Old Testament as evidence that this meaning of *kephale* was familiar to Greek-speaking people in New Testament times.

However, the facts do not support that argument. About 180 times in the Old Testament, the Hebrew word *ro'sh* (head) is used with the idea of chief, leader, superior rank (similar to the way English-speaking people use "head"). However, those who translated the Hebrew Old Testament into Greek (between 250 and 150 B.C.) rarely used *kephale* (head) when the Hebrew word for head carried this idea of leader, chief, or authority. They usually used the Greek word *archon,* meaning leader, ruler, or commander. They also used other words. In only 17 places (out of 180) did they use *kephale,* although that would have been the simplest way to translate it. Five of those 17 have variant readings, and another 4 involve a head-tail metaphor that would make no sense without the use of head in contrast to tail. That leaves only 8 instances (out of 180 times) when the Septuagint translators clearly chose to use *kephale* for *ro'sh* when it had a "superior rank" meaning. Most are in relatively obscure places.

Since *kephale* is so rarely used when *ro'sh* carried the idea of authority, most of the Greek translators apparently realized that *kephale* did not carry the same "leader" or "superior rank" meaning for "head" as did the Hebrew word *ro'sh.*

There are seven passages in the New Testament where Paul uses *kephale* in some figurative sense. The concept of a hierarchy, with men in a role of authority over women (at least over their wives) rests largely on two of these: 1 Corinthians 11:3 and Ephesians 5:23. When Paul used *kephale* in these two passages, was he thinking of one of the usual Greek meanings of head, or a common figurative Hebrew meaning?

Paul knew both Hebrew and Greek. Although he was a Pharisee who knew Hebrew well, he grew up in Tarsus, a Greek-speaking city. Greek was his native tongue. In all the passages where he used *kephale,* he was writing to Greek-speaking people in cities where most Christians were converts from Greek religions. Their contact with the Old Testament would be limited to hearings parts of the Septuagint read in their services. They might go to church for years without ever hearing those eight relatively obscure places in the Greek Old Testament where *kephale* seemed to have a different meaning from the usual meanings in their own language.

Since Paul was Greek-speaking Jew, he would likely write to Greek-speaking Christians using Greek words with Greek meanings they would easily understand.

If "head" in Greek did not normally mean "supreme over" or "authority over," what did it mean in those seven New Testament passages where Paul used it figuratively? Careful examination of context shows that common Greek meanings not only make good sense, but present a more exalted Christ.

1. Colossians 1:18 (context 1:14-20); *kephale* means "exalted originator and completer." "He (Christ) is the head of the body, the church; he is the beginning, the firstborn from the dead, that in everything he might be preeminent." Paul seems to be using *kephale* with common Greek meanings—"source or beginning or completion" (Liddell, Scott, et al.)—in a sense that Christ is the exalted originator and completer of the church. Bauer does not list this passage among those where *kephale* means "superior rank."

2. Colossians 2:19 (context 2:16-19); *kephale* means "source of life." Christ is the source of life who nourishes the church.

Christians are told to hold fast to Christ, who is described as the "head," from whom the whole body, nourished and knit together through its joints and ligaments, grows with a growth that is from God. Bauer agrees that in this passage *kephale* does not mean "superior rank."

3. Ephesians 4:15 (context 4:11-16) is very similar to Colossians 2:19. It reads, "We are to grow up in every way into him who is the head, into Christ, from whom the whole body, joined and knit together by every joint with which it is supplied, when each part is working properly, makes bodily growth and upbuilds itself in love." This passage stresses the unity of head and body, and presents Christ as the nourisher and source of growth. Bauer classifies *kephale* here as meaning "superior rank," although he does not see that meaning in the very similar Colossians 2:19.

4. 1 Corinthians 11:3 (context 11:2-16); *kephale* seems to carry the Greek concept of head as "source, base, or derivation." "Now I want you to realize that the head of every man is Christ, and the head of the woman is man, and the head of Christ is God" (NIV). In this passage Paul is discussing how men and women should pray and prophesy in public church meetings. His instructions apparently relate to the customs, dress, and lifestyle in Corinth and the tendency of the Corinthian believers to be disorderly. Paul discusses women's and men's head coverings and hair styles. (Veils are not mentioned in the Greek text.) Paul says, "man was not made from woman, but woman from man" (v. 8); he also says, "woman was made from man" (v. 12). This suggests that Paul used "head" in verse 3 with the meaning of "source or origin." Man was the "source or beginning" of woman in the sense that woman was made from the side of Adam. Christ was the one through whom all creation came (1 Cor. 8:6b). God is the base of Christ (John 8:42: "I proceeded and came forth from God").

129

When we recognize one Greek meaning of *kephale* as a source or origin, as Paul explains in verses 8 and 12, then verse 3 does not seem to teach a chain of command. Paul's word order also shows he was not thinking of chain of command: Christ, head of man; man, head of woman; God, head of Christ. Those who make it a chain of command must rearrange Paul's words. In fact, Paul seems to go out of his way to show that he was not imputing authority to males when he says, "For as woman was made from man, so man is now born of woman. And all things are from God" (1 Cor. 11:12).

5. Ephesians 5:23 (context 5:18-23); "head" is used in a head-body metaphor to show the unity of husband and wife and of Christ and the church. "For the husband is head of the wife as Christ is the head of the church, his body." Paul often used the head-body metaphor to stress the unity of Christ and the church. In fact, this unity forms the context for this passage. The head and body in nature are dependent on each other.

This verse follows Paul's explanation of what it means to be filled with the Holy Spirit. His last instruction is, "Be subject to one another out of reverence for Christ" (v. 21). This is addressed to all Christians and obviously includes husbands and wives. Naturally, as part of this mutual submission of all Christians to each other, wives are to submit to their husbands.

The Greek word "submit" or "be subject to" does not appear in verse 22. It says only, "wives to your husbands." The verb supplied must therefore refer to the same kind of submission demanded of all Christians in verse 21.

To stress the oneness of husband and wife, Paul then returns to his favorite head-body metaphor: "For the husband is the head *(kephale)* of the wife as Christ is the head *(kephale)* of the church, his body."

Paul develops his head-body metaphor at length in 1 Corinthians 12:22-27. If he thought of "head" as the part of the body that had authority over the rest of it, would not that meaning appear in this long passage? We know that the brain controls the body. But Paul did not use that concept in his metaphor. He refers to the ears, eyes, and nose; the head as a whole is mentioned only in verse 21: "The eye cannot say to the hand, 'I have no need of you,' nor again the head to the feet, 'I have no need of you.' " Paul taught here the unity and mutual dependence of all parts on each other: "If one member suffers, all suffer together, if one member is honored, all rejoice together" (v. 26). There is no suggestion that the head has authority over other parts of the body.

Christ does have authority over the church (Matt. 16:18). But most of the passages that deal with Christ as the head of the church do not point to his authority over the church, but rather the oneness of Christ and the church. In Ephesians 5:18-33, this oneness is applied to husband and wife.

If we are to see a meaning in "head" in Ephesians 5:23 beyond the head-body metaphor of mutual dependence and unity, we must do so on the basis of the immediate context. Christ's headship of the church is described like this: "Christ loved the church and gave himself up for her" (v. 25). Christ gave himself up to enable the church to become all that it is meant to be—holy and without blemish.

As Christ is the enabler (the one who brings to completion) of the church, so the husband is to enable (bring to completion) all that his wife is meant to be. The husband is to nourish and cherish his wife as he does his own body, even as Christ nourishes and cherishes the church (v. 29).

The concept of sacrificial self-giving so that a spouse can achieve full potential has been the role that society has traditionally given to the wife. Here Paul gives it to the husband. Of course, giving oneself sacrificially for the other is an excellent example of the submission wives and husbands are to have toward each other (v. 21).

6. Ephesians 1:20-23 (context 1:13-23); *kephale* means "top or crown." Paul presents an exalted picture of Christ and his authority over everything in creation: ". . . when he raised him from the dead and made him sit at his right hand in the heavenly places, far above all rule and authority and power and dominion, and above every name that is named, not only in this age, but also in that which is to come; and he has put all things under his feet and has made him the head over all things for the church, which is his body, the fulness of him who fills all in all." The authority of Christ, established in verses 20-21, is extended to every extremity from crown (head) to feet—including the church which is his body.

7. Colossians 2:10 (context 2:8-15); *kephale* again seems to have the Greek idea of life-source, as well as the idea of top or crown. This verse emphasizes the church as the "fulness" of Christ. "For in him the whole fulness of deity dwells bodily, and you have come to fulness of life in him, who is the head of all rule and authority" (vv. 9-10).

Paul uses two metaphors here—the head-body metaphor, with the church coming to "fulness of life" in Christ (the life-source, nourisher, enabler), and also the concept of top or crown when he speaks of Christ as the head of all rule and authority. In these two passages, "top" or "crown" emphasize Christ's position by virtue of the cross and resurrection. He is the victor, and is crowned with glory and honor (Heb. 2:9; Ps. 8:5).

These are the only passages in the New Testament where *kephale* is used figuratively. They include the five given by Bauer as examples of *kephale* meaning "superior rank," despite the fact that such a meaning for *kephale* does not appear in the secular Greek of New Testment times. If Paul had been thinking about authority, or leader, there were easily understood Greek words he could have used, and which he did use in other places. He used *exousia* (authority) in Romans 13:1-2; and *archon* Romans 13:3.

The passages where Paul used *kephale* in a figurative way make better sense and present a more exalted, completed view of Christ when *kephale* is read with recognized Greek meanings that would have been familiar to his original readers. Among these meanings are: exalted originator and completor; source, base, derivation; enabler (one who brings to completion); source of life; top or crown.

Can we legitimately read an English or Hebrew meaning into the word "head" in the New Testament, when both context and secular Greek literature of New Testament times seem to indicate that "superior rank" or "authority over" were not meanings that Greeks associated with the word, and probably were not the meanings the apostle Paul had in mind? Has our misunderstanding of some of these passages been used to support the concept of male dominance that has ruled most pagan and secular societies since the beginning of recorded history? Has this misunderstanding also robbed us of the richer, more exalted picture of Christ that Paul was trying to give us?

14

More on New Testament Headship

The Mickelsens gave us a rich source of information in their article reprinted in chapter thirteen. However, several questions surfaced that must be satisfactorily answered before the fog surrounding the woman-in-ministry question settles. Therefore, this chapter will add to what they have already said. Since this is a radical departure from the traditional meaning of *kephale* and the subjugation of women, I want to break the flow of this study and inject the *Eight Rules of Interpretation* used by legal experts for more than 2500 years.

1. *Rule of Definition.* Define the term of words being considered and then adhere to the defined meanings.

2. *Rule of Usage.* Don't add meanings to established words and terms. What was the common usage in the cultural and time period when the passage was written?

3. *Rule of Context.* Avoid using words out of context. Context must define terms and how words are used.

4. *Rule of Historical Background.* Don't separate interpretation and historical investigation.

5. *Rule of Logic.* Be certain that words as interpreted agree with the overall premise.

6. *Rule of Precedent.* Use the known and commonly accepted meanings of words, not obscure meanings for which there is no precedent.

7. *Rule of Unity.* Even though many documents may be used there must be a general unity among them.

8. *Rule of Inference.* Base conclusions on what is already known and proven or can be reasonably implied from all known facts.

It will be worth your time to acquaint yourself with these rules and commit them to memory or jot them in the flyleaf of your Bible. Using them will keep you free from cultism and false teachings. All the early Church Fathers used them. Irenaeus used them when he wrote *Against Heresies,* which dealt with Gnosticism and other untruths. Luther used them to refute religious fallacies of his day. Every law court religiously follows them and honest theologians dare not violate them. Much false teaching is the result of violating one or more of these universal rules of interpretation.

Back to 1 Corinthians 11. Thousands of words have been spoken and written trying to explain what Paul meant, yet this passage remains one of the most perplexing in the Scriptures. At least three reasons are given for its difficulty. First, Paul used some Greek words that aren't common to the rest of the New Testament, making it difficult to compare them in context and usage. Second, he discussed customs and practices that are foreign and vague to us today, leaving us partially ignorant of the historical background. Third, he answered questions they asked him and we don't know what those questions were. It's like listening to someone talk on the phone and trying to guess what the other person is saying.

Paul prefaced his answer by commending the Corinthians for keeping the traditions *(paradosis)* just as he delivered them (11:1-2). *Paradosis* is the same word Jesus used in Matthew 15:2 to describe the hand-me-down teachings of the rabbis. It's possible these traditions were peculiar to this church since the Church of Christ isn't founded upon traditions but the Word of God. Perhaps Paul had in mind the Lord's supper or baptism, but these are not mentioned in the passage. The use of the word "ordinances" in the King James Version is unfortunate since the uninformed reader assumes these instructions are comparable to and included with the other church ordinances such as baptism.

However, verse 16 casts doubt on this idea: "But if one is inclined to be contentious, we have no other practice, nor have the churches of God." What practice was he talking about? The practice of being contentious? That isn't a practice, it's a sin of the flesh (Gal. 5:20). Was it the practice of rebellious females not recognizing the "headship" of their husbands? This idea is foreign to the context. The suggestion that long-haired men were defending short-haired, unveiled women is also moot. History informs us most Christian women continued wearing the covering during the early days of the infant church. Further, there isn't any logical Christian doctrine or reason why women should cover their heads except to pattern themselves after the world. The Christian church isn't governed by the Talmudic interpretations of the Jewish rabbis, so this suggestion is irrelevant. Neither are Christians governed by the social customs of their society. The most logical conclusion is that the other churches didn't have long-haired men who wore a covering in public church services.

The Problem in Corinth

This chapter is filled with so many different ideas that it's easy to miss the main message. The ideas of headship, veiling, covering, woman's submission, long or short hair and angelic authority are intriguing aspects of Paul's primary purpose: to show how men and women may worship in a way glorifying God (10:31). The hierarchy of men and women isn't a major consideration but it has been made one. A careful study of the whole passage poses this question: "Why can't men wear a covering as the women do?"

Jewish men wore the *tallith,* a small head covering symbolizing their guilt and unworthiness before a Holy God. It's a humble gesture, based not on a biblical command, but on a rabbinical "law."

What Was the Covering?

This is an integral part of the question. Leonard Swidler's informative book, *Women in Judaism,* quotes the oral law and Billerbeck: "Jewish women in Palestine before and after the Common Era, and probably also later in Babylonia, always appear in public with their head and face largely covered. The head and face covering probably consisted of a plaited hair-do combined with two kerchiefs, a forehead band with ribbons and bows on it . . . Here one can see clearly that the covering and the veiling of the woman consisted of her coiffure."[1] Remember our study in chapter three, "As Also Saith the Law," on how Jewish women appeared in public and the reason they were covered.

Knowing what the covering was makes Paul's statement that a woman's long hair was given to her for a covering sensible (11:15). His transition from covering to hair has caused more commentators to assume the hair was the place for the covering. Actually, the Greek text reads "because the long hair instead of a covering has been given to her." Verse 14 flows out of the previous statement which says, "Does not even nature itself teach you that if a man has long hair, it is a dishonor to him?"

Does nature teach us that long hair on men is shameful? Does nature give men short hair and women long hair? It's the barber who makes hair short. Was Jesus shamed because His hair was long? Since the woman traditionally wore a covering, and since long hair was given to them instead of a covering, should men not cover their heads for the same reasons? All the unfruitful arguments about veils, hats, shawls, and bonnets are irrelevant. Women's hair didn't need covering with something else; her hair was the covering.

Why Were the Women Covered?

Paul said men should not cover their heads, so why did he allow women to cover theirs? If the New Covenant freed Jewish men from their customs, didn't it also free Jewish women from the same customs? This is probably the question the Corinthians asked Paul in their letter to him: "Why may the women wear their covering but we have to discard ours?" Because each sex wore them for different reasons. Men covered their heads to symbolize their guilt and unworthiness before the law while women covered their heads (and faces) because they were guilty and unworthy before men.

Many Christian women were still married to orthodox Jews whose laws demanded an immediate divorce from any woman who disobeyed the law by appearing in public uncovered.[2] An uncovered woman was looked upon as unchaste. Dr. Alfred Edersheim, in *Sketch of Jewish Social Life,* wrote, "It was the custom in case of a woman accused of adultery to have her hair shorn or shaven."[3] Therefore, a Jewish husband, even though not against his wife's Christian commitment, would be compelled by the synagogue authorities to divorce his wife if she was seen in public with her hair not done up. So Paul argued, "Go along with the custom!"

By way of argument, if Paul was demanding the veiling of women, why does history reveal that the women "sat unveiled in the assemblies in a separate place, by the presbyters," and were "ordained by the laying on of hands," until the Church Council of Laodicea forbade it in 363?[4]

Remember that, according to Jewish theology, one of the ten curses laid on Eve and her descendants was the covering of her face and head all the days of her life. So both men and women were covered in Corinth, but for two different reasons. One was a social and religious custom, while the other was based on unworthiness. Thank God, man no longer stands in God's presence shaking in fear, guilt and shame, but as a son of God clothed in Christ's rightousness (Rom. 8:1). That's why Paul frowned on the male covering: It dishonored man's head, Christ, the source, origin and sustainer of life. But Paul, in permitting the women to cover their heads, was not labelling them unworthy; he was only requiring them to conform to the contemporary rules of decorum.

Does this mean Christian women must cover their heads? If they want to; it's a matter of personal choice, not scriptural ordinance. Jewish women wore a covering, believing Eve was the cause of sin and death. But we know that woman was not the cause of sin, so why should she be humiliated as though she were guilty? But what about the teaching that the covering is a sign that she has submitted to her husband?

Does Woman Need a Covering?

In recent years a new theory on the "covering" has surfaced; namely, that a covering represents a chain-of-command. Christ is the Church's covering. The Church is man's covering, while man is the woman's covering. If a woman is single, an elder must be provided or appointed as her covering. Each person must submit to someone over him in the hierarchy of

Church authority. "Who is your covering?" is a frequently asked question among subscribers to this theory.

It's true each believer and each ministry should be under the authority of a church, but the Scriptures don't call this relationship a covering, nor does 1 Corinthians 11:1-16 provide the slightest hint that the covering included a veil of authority over every believer.

A Heady Hierarchy

The Jehovah's Witnesses believe in and practice the total submission of women to men under a strict hierarchy. In their *Aid to Bible Understanding,* a dictionary-commentary containing their interpretation of the Bible, under the article "Headship" they quote 1 Corinthians 11:3 to support their version of male supremacy and female submission. "The apostle Paul, drawing on the principle of primary headship of God, the head of Christ, and the relative headship of man over woman, set forth the principle governing the Christian congregation."[5]

As I stated in chapter seven, the Jehovah's Witnesses teach that Jehovah God created Jesus as His first and only direct act of creation. To them there isn't any doubt— Jehovah God is unquestionably Christ's head, since He created Him. In like manner, they regard man as woman's head since she was made from his side. In this sense he was her source of being the same way the Logos came out of God. Actually, they have two gods, the Almighty God who created a mighty god, Jesus, the Word. Naturally, that which is created is subservient to the One who created it. If Christ had had a beginning, God the Father would indeed be His Lord. However, Christians can't use this line of reasoning. We know that within the Godhead there are three co-equal and co-eternal persons ruling as co-regents.

How Was God Christ's Head?

We know that the Son proceeds from the Father (John 1:14), and that the man Jesus had His origin in the Godhead (Luke 1:35). He was conceived by the Spirit of God in the womb of a virgin and called the Son of God (Luke 1:32). God was the source, origin, and nourisher of His life.

"And the Word was God" (John 1:1). In the very beginning Jesus, the Logos, was eternal God. There is no priority here: He was face-to-face with God *(ho theos* or God the Father). He was and is God, part of the Source and exactly like the original Source. "And He is the radiance of His glory and the exact representation of His nature, and upholds all things by the word of His power" (Heb. 1:3). In other words, because Jesus is equal to the Source, and God the Father is the Source, Jesus and God the Father are equal to each other! Christ has always had His being in God. Christ was in God the same way God was in Christ reconciling the world unto himself (Col. 2:9). They are one. There never was a time when any person in the Godhead was greater than the others except during the brief time Jesus was a man on earth. Within the Godhead there is mutual submission, mutual authority, mutual unity and oneness beyond human comprehension.

How Is Man the Head of a Woman?

Paul used two different words for "man" in his statement in 1 Corinthians 11:3: "But I would have you know, that the head of every man [*andros*] is Christ; and the head . . . of the woman is the man [*aner*]" (KJV). *Andros* comes from *aner,* a word meaning man, husband or male. Christ is head of both male and female who are part of His body. John Chrysostom, second-century scholar, said, "He cannot be the Head of those who are not in the Body . . . so when he says 'of every man' one must understand it of believers."

When Paul referred to the man as "head" of not "women" but "a woman" *(gunaikos)*, the word changed from *andros* to *aner,* meaning adult male or husband. The oral law stated the *aner* alone was obliged to wear the *tallith* or head covering. At best the husband is the head of his wife; this excludes other women in the congregation.

How is man the head of a woman? Not by exercising final authority over her, making her decisions, giving her permission to pray and prophesy, or insisting on "headship" as his scriptural position.

Jesus said, "You know that those who are recognized as rulers of the Gentiles lord it over them; and their great men exercise authority over them. But it is not so among you, but whoever wishes to become great among you shall be your servant" (Mark 10:42-43). What a powerful word! This one statement should make every bossy believer think. The Gentiles exercise authority and demand obedience but Christians must not. Why?

Paul described the most powerful force in the universe as godly love, *agape* (1 Cor. 13). Among the marvelous qualities mentioned by the apostle are these: "[It] does not act unbecomingly; it does not seek its own [way]."

How can a loving husband exercise authority over his wife, expecting and demanding her submission, when the love of Christ doesn't seek its own way? A husband filled with godly love wants to please his wife rather than himself. Some argue, "But this authority is delegated and he must exercise it to fulfill his duty!" This authority is not delegated. It is assumed by man's carnality! What husband wants to dominate his wife if he loves her as much as his own body? If anything, love works just the opposite.

A husband and wife filled with the love of Christ together approach the real authority in their family and ask Him what He wants; together they fulfill His will. If a husband's desire is the Lord's will, his wife will go along with it gladly. But if a husband makes the final word his own, she will rebel every time. Why? Because sin and carnality have taken over.

Husband and wife are joint heirs of eternal life; both of them are born-again creatures in Christ. Both have been delivered from the powers of darkness into the Kingdom of the Son. Together they stand in His Majesty's presence without guilt, fear or condemnation, clothed in the righteousness of Christ. Side by side they stand at the foot of His cross. Is this true only in the spiritual realm? In the physical realm, is man still supreme?

As a man is spiritually so he is physically. Being equal in the family of God spiritually will affect a husband and wife physically. Attitudes, goals, purposes and relationships will be tempered by their spiritual life. What person walking in God's love has any desire to have his own way, the last word, or the final decision? As believers we are equal in Christ (Gal. 3:28). The purpose of the New Creation is to lift both men and women into the heavenly places where mutual acceptance is the norm. Christ has redeemed us from the curse of the law and restored us to humanity's original position with God (Gen. 1:26, 27). Paul used this analogy as a basis for arguing against men covering their heads during public worship.

After telling them they all have their source of life in Christ the head, he drew a clear line of distinction between men and women. The Jewish men knew why women wore coverings—because Eve was made from Adam to be his helper and because she sinned—so Paul reminded them in 1 Corinthians 11:8 that man did not originate or come from a woman but woman from man. In Jewish custom, women were covered because they were weak, inferior and easily deceived. Why should a man cover his head if he is the strong one, the superior one?

After using Jewish Talmudic theology and putting the women in their place, he didn't leave them there since that argument was Jewish, not Christian. This can be seen with his "However, in the Lord," in verse 11. This completely changes the complexion of the argument. "However, in the Lord" defuses any possibility of his previous statement being taken out of context. Women were covered because the oral law required it. "However, in the Lord" it isn't this way!

"For as the woman originates [or comes from] the man, so also the man has his birth through the woman; and all things originate from God" (11:12).

This verse strengthens the thought that *kephale* has the meaning of "source, origin, sustainer." The literal Greek, "For as the woman *of* the man, so also the man *through* the woman; but all things *of* God." The same way woman is of the man, all things are of God!

Any previous distinction or special position man enjoyed before the birth of the first child was removed by this verse since all men have their life, origin and birth through a woman. If that which precedes is superior to that which came after, then every mother is head of any son to whom she gave birth! The equalizer is the apostle's statement: "And all things originate from God." God made the man and He made the woman, and He still makes both by using procreation; how can anyone say one is superior to the other since both are from God? Which one is first in line to be the leader? The truth is, Paul wasn't talking first or second, leader or follower, authority or submission, but why men shouldn't cover their heads during public worship in Christian assemblies. He didn't give *kephale* an obscure meaning but used the meaning commonly accepted by his listeners.

In conclusion, his final statement was "the other churches of God don't follow these traditions."

Chapter Fourteen Notes

1. Leonard Swidler, *Women in Judaism* (Metuchen, NJ: Scarecrow Press, 1976), pp. 122-123.
2. *Babylonian Talmud,* Kethuboth, 6, 6.
3. Alfred Edersheim, *Sketch of Jewish Social Life* (Grand Rapids, MI: Eerdmans, 1974), p. 155.
4. Katherine Bushnell, *God's Word to Women* (1923; privately reprinted by Ray Munson, N. Collins, NY), p. 244.
5. *Aid to Bible Understanding* (Brooklyn, NY: Watch Tower Tract and Bible Society, 1971). p. 724.

15

Women, Submission and Christ

> For the husband is the head of the wife, as Christ
> also is the head of the church, He Himself being the
> Savior of the body (Eph. 5:23).

This is the most used scripture teaching the wife's
submission, as well as the last *kephale* allegory Paul used.
It isn't the purpose of this study to explore the family
relationship, but it must be briefly touched on since
the husband-wife relationship is a type of Christ and the
Church.

Again *kephale* is used in a figurative sense. If Paul
had wanted to teach male authority, this was his opportunity.
He could have used either the Greek word *archon* or *exousia,*
both meaning authority or domination, and there would
have been no question. It seems doubtful he would have
concealed such an important function in strange, metaphorical
language. For an in-depth study of "headship," read Stephen
Bedale's "The Meaning of Kephale in the Pauline Epistles"[1] or
Kittel and Friedrich's *Theological Dictionary of the New
Testament.*[2]

Some Interpretations of Paul's Advice

Charles Hodge, Calvinist theologian, wrote concerning this verse that women's subjugation is religious as unto the Lord. He said, "Man is stronger, larger, bolder; has more of those mental and moral qualities which are required of a leader. This superiority is founded in nature."[3] I dare not criticize Dr. Hodge since he wrote more than a century ago, but studies and facts today refute his thesis. Some men are larger, stronger and morally superior to some women, but not to all. Some women are far superior to many men. The facts negate his assumption.

George Knight, in *The New Testament Teaching on the Role Relationship of Men and Women,*[4] also embraced the submission of women both in and out of church. While Hodge viewed submission as religious, Knight saw it as a total role, basing his thesis on the idea that headship and submission is a divine ordinance. "The evidence that the apostles root the uniform teaching about headship and submission for husband and wife in the creation order of God surfaces in the quote from Genesis 2:24 and Ephesians 5:31. *We must admit that Genesis 2:24 seems to surface only in Ephesians 5:31* [emphasis mine]. Clearly, Genesis 2 truths are the basis for the apostle's consistent teaching about headship and submission."[5]

Mr. Knight based his entire evidence on one verse that seems to surface only in Ephesians 5:31. To say the teaching is uniform apostolic teaching is misleading since only Paul touched this subject. One apostle's teaching doesn't make it uniform apostolic doctrine. Further, Knight's assumption is based on one verse, Genesis 2:24, which has been analyzed thoroughly. There isn't anything in that verse to imply that because man was made first he was the leader. Man and woman were co-regents, not one following the other. His admission that this verse is the only basis for the authority-submission roles is alarming. If his interpretation is wrong, so are his conclusions. Was woman created to submit?

Peter Brunner in *The Ministry and the Ministry of Women* upheld the ontological thesis that God created women to submit. John MacArthur approached this passage with a different slant: since Eve usurped Adam's authority and acted independently, submission was her "curse." "Therefore Genesis 3:16 would rightly read, To the woman He said . . . your desire will be to control your husband, but he will rule you."[6] If I've misread or misjudged these men I beg their forgiveness, but it appears they were enforcing a practice based upon one huge assumption applied to two Scriptures.

Is it right to use the Bible to perpetuate the rejection of women in ministry the same way the church once used the Scriptures to defend slavery?

Those who reject women in ministry explain the allegory like this: The wife (body) submits to her husband (head), fulfilling his will (he always has the last word whether right or wrong) the same way the Church (body) submits to Christ (head). As the Church is subject to Christ, so wives should be subject to their husbands in everything.

What Does Submission Mean?

Ephesians 5:21 says, ". . . be subject to one another in the fear of Christ." In verse 18 Paul told them to be filled and stay filled with the Holy Spirit. How were they to remain Spirit-filled? By keeping a joyful heart, a praising mouth and a grateful attitude, basic elements in all relationships. The rest of chapter 5 and most of chapter 6 tell us how this submission can be expressed. First husbands and wives, then children and parents, then slaves and masters. Paul used the verb *hupotasso,* which comes from the simple verb *tasso,* meaning "I arrange," and *hupo,* "next after," or "under." Originally, it was a military term describing the submission of subordinates to superiors as soldiers line up, row after row, behind their leaders. However, the noun *hupotage* (subjection or submission) isn't found outside the New Testament. Most language experts assume Paul coined it especially for New Testament believers.

The verb *hupotasso* in its active form means to "put in subjection" or "arrange after" but it is only used of the believer's relationship to God the Father or the Lord Jesus Christ. They alone can demand your submission. But when referring to relationships among believers, Paul used the middle voice, which has the meaning to "submit our control," or "yield." It's the opposite of self-assertion, independence or aggressiveness. It's the desire to get along with one another, and of the thirty-four times it's used in the Scriptures, only four of them deal with marital relationships. *Hupotasso* never means obey nor is the word obedience used of the husband-wife role.

Hupotasso is a Christian virtue void of the meaning of delegated subjugation; rather, it means a willing submission. It is never forced, compulsory or demanded; it is always voluntary and motivated by *agape* love. *Hupotasso* is a Spirit-filled, Spirit-controlled believer taking the second seat rather than the first, submitting to others rather than lording it over others. It's having the mind of Christ. Philippians 2:6-7 says, "Who, being in the form of God, thought it not robbery to be equal with God: But made himself of no reputation, and took upon him the form of a servant, and was made in the likeness of men"(KJV). Most church problems begin when someone wants to be first, have his own way, insist on his rights or demand recognition.

Mutual submission is not interpreted, guided or motivated by the structures of society or the practices of non-Christian philosophies. It is so intertwined with *agape* love that the two can't be separated. In other words, without *agape* there can't be Christian *hupotasso* since the latter is the natural working out of love in mutual submission. Further, *hupotasso* can be understood only in terms of the coming of the Holy Spirit since it flows out of being Spirit-filled (Eph. 5:18-21). From this we may conclude that husbands and wives under the Old Covenant knew nothing about *hupotasso.*

The Principle of Submission

Paul's exhortation includes all believers, male and female, husbands and wives. There isn't one kind of submission for those in the church and another kind for wives. As Spirit-filled believers, as fellow disciples, husbands submit to their wives as well as to other believers: "And be subject to one another in the fear of Christ." Together, the husband and wife yield to the rest of the church. It is this mutual submission and mutual acceptance that releases the mighty power of the Spirit when the Body is gathered together. "Where two or three have gathered together in My name, there I am in their midst," Jesus said. Being Spirit-filled burns away any desire to act on your own or have your own way. Every member of the church mutually submits to every other member. That is *hupotasso.*

Paul said, "Wives, be subject to your own husbands, as to the Lord" (Eph. 5:22). In Colossians, he worded it differently: "Wives, be subject to your husbands, as is fitting in the Lord" (3:18). In both passages the wives' submission is to be in accordance with what is acceptable to the Lord—it is not a blanket order. The verb "be subject," is italicized in most English translations since it isn't in the original manuscripts. Ephesians 5:22 has no verb. It says, "Wives, to your own husbands." How did this sentence fragment happen? Before the Greek text was translated and divided into numbered verses with paragraphs and chapters it was one continual sentence without punctuation or paragraphs. Therefore, there was no break between verses 21 and 22. Both were part of the same statement, so the verb in verse 21 is the verb controlling verse 22. It should read, "Be in mutual submission to one another in the fear of Christ; wives to your own husbands, as to the Lord."

Although commentators and teachers have made the woman's submission the focal point of these verses, with the emphasis on verse 22, this wasn't Paul's main theme or purpose. Mutual submission is the context of his teaching. A Spirit-filled wife yields to her husband the same way she yields to every other member of the church body and in the same manner the husband submits to his wife. This was the heart of Paul's teaching, in opposition to the Judaizers, who still dominated their women. They were the ones arguing for the silencing of women in Corinth (1 Cor. 14:34-35). So Paul boldly equated the wife's new role in Christ with her husband's. Some teachers would explain: Even though there is mutuality, there is also authority and submission. Men and women are equal in essence but different in function. For the sake of the family, the woman submits, while her husband leads.

Even though this seems to be a practical, working relationship, I'm not aware of any Scripture substantiating the hierarchy. The New Testament, which is our covenant guidebook, has much to say about the family relationship but the only place that seemingly gives the husband priority is the passage from Ephesians 5. Throughout the New Testament the emphasis is always on mutual acceptance in Christian relationships as a result of being Spirit-filled. The idea that because man was created first the woman must be his helpmeet has already been studied in depth. The fact that Paul barely mentioned the wife's submission is significant. History accurately records women's role in subjugation. From the dawn of time they have been dominated by male strength. Female submission and male domination is all women had ever known, until Christianity delivered them.

I vividly remember the first time the Lord reminded me my wife was also my sister in Christ. I was pouting about something, I don't recall what, but probably because I couldn't have my own way. In those days I'd use a macho silent treatment and not talk. This particular time I sulked in the cellar of a Vermont country farm house where it was musty, damp and lonely. Just the right place for a pity party and for the Lord to get your attention.

"Don't forget your wife is also your sister. Would you treat another sister in the church that way?"

"No way! They pay tithes!"

"She's not only your wife and your sister, she's my personal disciple. Be careful how you treat her or you'll answer to me!"

It didn't take the Lord long to get through to me. I knew I was treading on thin ice. I ran upstairs with a new approach.

"Sister Trombley," I said piously, "as your pastor I'd like to talk with you." We've laughed about that many times but I began seeing a valuable truth.

In marriage, the wife is the husband's alter ego, the strength filling up his weaknesses, but she is also his neighbor and friend, and Jesus left some firm instructions about how a husband should treat her. "Love her as yourself!" What I'm saying is this: Christian *agape* love-submission is yielding, preferring one another without asserting personal rights!

I realize this doesn't agree with some modern marriage manuals telling wives to submit to all the demands of their husbands, in which husbands have the last word, right or wrong. One church was recently plagued by a problem that centered around the absolute authority of the husband and elders, who insisted on total submission. "Trust God as Sarah trusted the Lord," they argued. Such reverential obedience isn't Christian submission; it's creature worship; it's sin. Oh, that these teachers would have considered Paul's balancing words "in the Lord" or "as is fitting in the Lord." It might have mellowed their dictates, since only that which is acceptable to Christ is worth considering. Paul was not discussing submission between pagan husbands and wives, but between Christian mates. The grace of yielding is a direct result of being filled with the Spirit. Non-Christian submission is not the topic.

I cannot find any reputable lexicon suggesting that *hupotasso* conveys the thought of servile submission. Wives are not slaves. Submission, then, is a mutual function where one yields personal preferences to the other (where principles are not involved). It isn't a once-for-all act but an ongoing attitude, the result of being a new creature in Christ and Spirit-filled. I repeat, don't confuse submission with servility, or headship with lordship.

A word of caution is necessary here. Christ has absolute authority and control over His Church—the Church He purchased with His own blood and brought into existence by His resurrection. But His absolute authority isn't a function of His headship but of His lordship. When we confuse the function of "head" with the position as "lord," chaos follows. Both Christ and man are called heads, but man is never called lord. We obey Christ as our Lord, knowing He never demanded obedience or submission. He said, "If you love me, keep my commandments." If you don't love Him then you won't keep His commandments! He wants our obedience to be an expression of our love for Him. A man is never lord of anyone, including his wife, even though pagan gentiles do exercise authority and lordship over one another. Jesus said it would not be so among His disciples! Don't equate man's headship with Christ's lordship.

How Is Christ the Head of His Church?

Even as Eve was taken from the side of Adam, the church was birthed from the opened side of Christ on the cross. Without the shedding of His blood there would have been no "second Eve" called the Church. In this sense Eve was a type of the Church as Adam was a type of Christ. As the Church's source and sustaining life force, He nourishes and cherishes her (Eph. 5:29). It's His life that helps her reach maturity and attain the fullness of all she is ordained to become (Eph. 4:12-16). Christ is described as the cornerstone, the headstone, holding the building together (Ps. 118:22; Eph. 2:20). Remove the cornerstone and the building collapses. In this sense He is the means of structural strength and unity.

As vibrant living stones, the church grows in Him as He ministers life and nourishment through the Word. Rather than insisting on His rightful place as Lord, He exalts His bride-church to be where He is, happily sharing His throne with her (Eph. 2:6). If she falls short, and she does, He doesn't reject her, but graciously edifies and comforts her until she ultimately reaches that goal (Phil. 1:6).

He is the conqueror who satisfactorily subdued Satan, sin, sickness and death. He alone is the mighty Master of all creation, but He lets His Church be *more* than a conqueror. Kenneth Copeland, television evangelist, illustrated it like this: A man trains, denies himself, suffers pain and physical abuse as he develops his skill in order to become a world champion heavyweight boxer. After many years of hard work, sacrifice and discipline and fifteen rounds of brutal punishment, he finally wins the coveted title: champion of the world. Later, with several million dollars as his financial reward, he goes home, elated! His hard work paid off! He has conquered every opponent he faced! His wife meets him at the door. She hasn't fought, much less trained for the fight, but she reaches out and takes the check. He's a conqueror, but she is more than a conqueror. He fought the fight and she received the benefits. That's exactly what my Jesus did!

His unselfish love for His church impelled Him to lay down His life for her redemption. He met the enemy head on; He entered the strong man's house and spoiled him by overcoming death. But not one act was done selfishly, for himself. Everything He did was for the Church. That's why she participates and shares His blessings (Eph. 1:3). She is so thoroughly saturated with His love that she is filled up with all the fullness of God (Eph. 3:17-19). All this is possible because Christ is the head, the cornerstone, the supplier of the necessary life for her spiritual development (Eph. 4:15-16).

This is *hupotasso*, mutual submission. Christ gave himself as the source of our life, our head, but unless we submit to Him, there can't be perpetuation of that life. Of necessity we must cling to Him as He clings to us. We desperately need Him—without Him we are nothing—but neither can He do anything without us. That's why Paul used Genesis 2:24 as an illustration. Genesis 2:24 says nothing about man exercising authority over his wife or having the last word. It does say he must leave his father and mother and cling to his wife. There must be mutual yielding or there can't be any reproduction. As head, man has the seed, the life source, but woman has the ovum, a complementary and necessary life source.

How Does the Husband Submit to His Wife?

Having briefly mentioned the wife's act of submission, Paul then gave detailed instructions for the husband (Eph. 5:25-33). Although the role of the woman had been the sacrificial self-giver, the apostle now explained how the husband's part in mutual submission works. Even as the wife willingly gives herself to her husband, so her husband also gives himself to her.

Such a revolutionary idea must have devastated the Judaizers. Within Judaism the husband wasn't responsible for his wife's spiritual or intellectual development. Her voice was considered distasteful, her presence distracting, and her intelligence inferior. Women were not allowed to study the Torah or required to fulfill its precepts. But as new creatures in

Christ, the sexual, national and social barriers were broken down (Gal. 3:28). Paul promoted a radical change in the way husbands accepted their wives. Wives had always submitted to their husbands, but now the husbands had to begin submitting, too.

How does the husband submit to his wife? By accepting her and treating her exactly as Christ loves His Church. The same love the Lord has for His people is the same love husbands must show their wives. Four times Paul told husbands to love their wives, with *agape* love, but he never used *agape* to tell wives how to love their husbands. *Agape* love is that quality of selfless, sacrificial and submissive love that expects nothing in return.

"Gladys!" I said to my wife. "It isn't fair. Men do all the lovin' and women do all the gettin'." Then she shared something with me I've never forgotten.

"That's because you don't have to tell a woman to love her husband as a command; it's her desire. When her husband loves her as selflessly as Christ loved the Church, she knows it. One doesn't have to tell a woman to love . . . it's as automatic as breathing. She knows when she's accepted and she knows when she feels used. When her husband willingly exalts her and genuinely loves her she will respond; it's her nature and has nothing to do with submission to authority. When you love someone you want to be one with them. Show me a man who selflessly loves his wife and I'll show you a truly happy woman."

In other words, when husbands love the Jesus way, wives submit the Jesus way. Without one, the other doesn't work. Everything we know about our Lord's humanity was self-emptying for the purpose of redemption. He was made flesh so man could become spiritual. He made himself nothing so we might become everything. He did nothing for himself, never insisted on having His own way or having the last word. Even the mighty name conferred upon Him when He ascended to the Father was given to His bride, the Church, as power of attorney. That's why Paul urged the Philippians to have the same mind as Christ (Phil. 2:5,6). Even as Christ left His Father's presence and joined himself to those who would become His bride, the husband forsakes his parents and joins himself to his wife. They forge a covenant in which she gives herself to him and he gives himself to her. He doesn't possess her and she doesn't possess him, since *agape* love isn't possessive but giving. Possessive love—and jealousy—aren't *agape* love but carnal selfishness. Instead, the new relationship of husband and wife involves mutual submission founded on selfless love.

How is man the head of his wife? Just as Christ personally brings His Church to perfection (Eph. 4:11-13), the husband helps his wife become all God wants her to be, so together they can be co-regents in life (Rom. 5:17). Unlike the Judaizers, who kept their women locked in ignorance, a Christian husband helps his wife develop. He cherishes her to the point where he gives his life to serve her. He helps her fulfill her desires and goals in life. He nourishes her as her source of strength and supply. He gives himself, as a Spirit-filled and Spirit-controlled believer, to her without reservation, expecting nothing in return but her personal fulfillment and happiness. He gives his all helping her reach new heights of spiritual and personal maturity.

As his body, as his own flesh, he carefully watches over her. The word *hos* (as) in Ephesians 5:28 means more than being similar. It has a qualitative force, meaning "as being." The head-body metaphor Paul used means that the relation of the "head" to the "body" makes the wife a vital part of the husband's self. To love his wife is to love himself, not out of duty but out of nature. Indeed, this teaching was foreign to Jewish men.

In the same way Christ and His Church are intimately one as a living organism, so husband and wife are intimately one. The two are one living organism, both growing, developing and maturing through and by the life source of God himself. Even as God said the man and woman would become one flesh (Gen. 2:24), so the husband and wife, redeemed from the curse of sin and death through the obedience of the Last Adam, become one flesh. Two separate persons, two different natures, two living beings become one new person. That's what being Spirit-filled means in Ephesians 5:18-20. Christ's Spirit dwelling in us gradually changes us into His likeness and image, restoring all that was lost through Adam's act of treason.

Whereas sacrificial self-giving had been solely the role of the woman, under the New Covenant, self-giving involves mutual submission as the husband learns how to yield to and become one with his wife. Previously the wife sacrificed her life helping the man reach his full potential, his goals and his desires. Paul assigned that same role to the husband, too. As her head he has the source of strength to make or break her. Both husband and wife should be Spirit-filled, and on that foundation, she submits to her husband as to the Lord. And on that same basis, the husband submits to her and God's desire for her. Together, they grow in Christ.

Chapter Fifteen Notes

1. *Journal of Theological Studies,* 5:212, 1954.
2. Volume 3 (Grand Rapids: Eerdmans), pp. 679-81.
3. Charles Hodge, *Epistle to the Ephesians.*
4. Grand Rapids, Baker Book House, 1979.
5. George Knight in *Christianity Today,* Feb. 20, 1982, p. 17.
6. John MacArthur, *Family Feuding and How to End It* (Panorama City, CA: Word of Grace Communications, 1981), p. 35.

16

Paul's Advice to Timothy

> But I do not allow a woman to teach or exercise authority over a man, but to remain quiet (1 Tim. 2:12).

This is the last and strongest Pauline statement keeping women out of the pulpit and in the pew. At the very least it seems to forbid them teaching when men are present or in authority.

Most Bible students agree this passage is one of the most frustrating in the Bible to understand and there are several reasons for the problem. In verse 10 Paul used a word for "professing godliness" which is not the regular word for confess or profess. It's a political expression he linked to improperly dressed women. In verse 12 he used a very rare Greek verb that was considered vulgar and isn't found anywhere else in the Scriptures. It is the word *authentein*, translated as "usurp authority" in the King James Version. Why didn't Paul use common words for "authority" or "usurp"? Did Paul disbar women from the teaching ministry even though he previously let them teach?

Susan Foh said Paul only kept the teaching and eldership from women, allowing women to have a say in the handling of funds, church property and the like. "There are no easy answers," she wrote.[1] Evidently she believed that women can teach since her book is a teaching medium. Whether that medium is the pulpit or the printed page, the result is the same: the body of Christ is edified. In spite of her hesitancy and "lack of easy answers," her conclusion is emphatic and final: women can't teach because of the creation order. If the creation order restricts women from teaching and eldership, why not in every area of life? Is there some correlation between man's creation and the pulpit? To be consistent, this logic should restrict women in every stratum of social and spiritual life and not just teaching and eldership. Adam wasn't created the first teaching elder but the first human.

Ms. Foh also said that many church offices have no scriptural basis. If these church positions aren't scriptural, why use the Scriptures to keep women out of them? She quoted three passages to substantiate her thesis (1 Cor. 11:2-16; 14:34, 35; 1 Tim. 2:11-14) and admitted they are difficult to understand. "Because of the difficulty, rather than wrestling with today's application of them, the church leaders take the prohibitions at their most comprehensive application just to make sure the commands are observed."[2] I wonder if these church leaders are as concerned about observing Paul's other clear commands such as "I want the men in every place to pray, lifting up holy hands" (1 Tim. 2:8) or "I wish that you all spoke in tongues" (1 Cor. 14:5). Many church leaders today would be scandalized if their men prayed with raised hands or in tongues just to make sure Paul's commands are being observed.

Why Paul Wrote to Timothy

Paul left his young friend in Ephesus to stop certain people from teaching strange doctrines, "that thou mightest charge some that they teach no other doctrine" (1 Tim. 1:3 KJV). "Some" comes from the Greek *tisin,* a neuter pronoun meaning either male or female. Observing Paul's exactness in the rest of his writings, I'm quite certain he would have said *aner* (men, as distinct from women) if he had been referring to a particular man or group of men. *Tisin* is a wide-open noun better translated as "certain persons."[3]

The word for the "strange doctrines" they taught comes from the Greek word meaning "a teacher of other than right doctrine, or playing the part of a teacher of other than right doctrine. One who holds opinions contrary to that which is orthodox."[4] Those people teaching strange doctrines dabbled in a mixture of myths and speculation, wanting to be teachers of the law (1 Tim. 1:7). A first impression points to the Judaizers again, but further study forbids this conclusion. Even if we change "myths" to "fables" (see 1 Tim. 4:7 or Titus 1:14), and "speculations" and "genealogies" (1 Tim. 1:4) to Jewish pedigrees, it doesn't answer all the questions. There isn't any evidence the Judaizers argued their family trees, and "myths" is a better translation than fables. Furthermore, early Christian writers closer to Paul than we are today used this passage to describe the Valentinians. Irenaeus applied this verse to the succession of Gnostic ages as did Tertullian who said, "The seeds of Gnostic heresies had already been sown in Paul's days." As we study this passage it becomes obvious he addressed the Gnostics rather than the Judaizers even though there seems to be some overlapping.

Paul's Battles With Heresies

Ephesus was a gentile metropolis and the church there was mostly gentile. Many of the converts, fresh out of paganism, held on to some of their former beliefs. Again and again Paul tackled the false teachings. His letters to Timothy and Titus, called the Pastoral Epistles, are often taught as a single unit because of their consistency in confronting heresy.[5]

That's why Paul told Titus to "reprove them severely that they may be sound in the faith" (Tit. 1:13). Don't pay "attention to Jewish myths and commandments of men who turn away from the truth" (v. 14). In this statement he linked myths and human commandments, implicating both Judaism and Gnosticism. He turned the heretics Hymenaeus and Philetus over to Satan for discipline, while Alexander the coppersmith was shut out of the church fellowship. Paul's stern instructions may be summed up in one phrase: "Stop all heretics from teaching!"

The Evidence of Gnosticism

Paul warned Timothy to "avoid worldly and empty chatter and the opposing arguments of what is falsely called 'knowledge'—which some have professed and thus gone astray from the faith" (1 Tim. 6:20, 21). This "knowledge" was the basis of Gnosticism. They claimed a hidden or secret knowledge *(gnosis),* hence their name. Paul's first letter to Timothy was written during the infancy of the Church when many of the heresies were still in the formative state, so not much is known about them from studying the Scriptures. That information came later when the Church Fathers, Clement of Alexandria (second century), Irenaeus (late second century), and Hippolytus (third century) wrote extensively about them. They identified some of the heretic leaders and gave detailed explanations of the strange teachers and rebutted them. Evidently, Paul confronted the formative errors while the later Church Fathers dealt with the full-blown heresies.

Some of the Gnostics claimed to be mediators between God and man and to possess secret truth. They taught detailed genealogies and myths about their beginnings, giving elaborate and exaggerated positions to Adam, Eve and others. Eve was exalted as the "bringer of life" to Adam, hence her name, "the mother of all living." When she ate of the tree of knowledge she allegedly received the hidden knowledge God had kept from them. Rather than calling her act sin, they exalted it as superiority. Even Hellenized Judaism taught female leadership based on Eve's "special knowledge." Philo of Alexandria, a first-century Jewish philosopher, allegorized the wives of Abraham, Isaac and Jacob as heavenly wisdom linked to man in a kind of sexual relationship. It was Gnosticism which brought to Christianity the concept of female mediators.

According to Hippolytus, the Priscillians esteemed Eve as their mediatrix, believing she received special knowledge from the serpent. Tertullian said they centered their entire theology around this point. The Nicolaitans, condemned by Jesus in Revelation 2:6, 15, believed Noah's wife wrote a sacred book.

Were There Women Among the Gnostic Leaders?

Extra-biblical writings say yes, but can we be sure? In 1 Timothy 5:11-15 and 2 Timothy 3:6-7 women are definitely implicated as those receiving false teaching, but who taught them? The context doesn't tell us, but the social structure of the day makes it doubtful that men were sneaking into the women's homes while their husbands were away. Paul called the teachings "profane" and "fit only for old women," a strong indication that women were the teachers. There isn't any doubt Jesus identified Jezebel as a false prophetess and teacher who taught heresies mixed with sexual immorality (Rev. 3:20). From the available information it can be deduced she was a Gnostic leader.

Foh argued, "The false teachers are not believers, and they live in immorality."[6] Her reasoning overlooked Paul's problem in Corinth. He addressed the Corinthians as saints (1 Cor. 1:2-8), even though he later said they were childish, immature, argumentative and immoral. One of them lived with his father's wife, an act that repulsed even the heathens, yet it was permitted by the church leaders. The proposition that the false teachers were not believers because they were immoral is not supported by Paul's first letter to the Corinthians.

The women in 1 Timothy 2:9-11 were teaching—"making a claim to godliness"—while the women in 2 Timothy 3:6-7 were the hearers—"always learning and never able to come to the knowledge of the truth." We can't assume the teachers were the same ones who entered the homes. But because these teachers aren't called immoral in 1 Timothy 2:9-11 doesn't mean they weren't false teachers.

A Conclusion Before We Begin

Here was the situation at Ephesus as I see it.

1. Gnostics were teaching strange doctrines (1:3-9).

2. Some of them claimed special knowledge (6:20).

3. These women promised godliness by means of good works (2:10).

4. They were unlearned and unskilled in the Word (1:1, 2:11). They had left the faith (2:15; 6:21).

5. Because they were unlearned and without faith, Paul didn't want them teaching (2:12) until they were qualified and properly taught.

6. Nor could they exercise their own brand of dominion over the man by using sexual power.

7. Paul scripturally refuted their claim to special knowledge by reminding them that Eve was made after the man and that she was deceived. His argument, as old as history, strips away any special glory Gnosticism gave Eve.

8. Finally, he gave hope to all women because of their uniqueness as mothers (2:15). If Adam's priority gave man preeminence over woman, then woman's priority over man comes through childbirth, now that man has his origin in woman.

Women Professing Godliness

>... but rather by means of good works, as befits
>women making a claim to godliness (2:10 NAS).

In most English versions verses 9 and 10 are parenthetical
and seem out of place. How does clothing relate to women
teaching? The key phrase is "professing godliness." On the
surface, "women professing godliness" gives the idea of a
public confession of faith or a public profession of conversion,
but this is an incorrect interpretation of this passage.

The common Greek word for "confession" or "profession" is
homologeo, and it's used many times. In Hebrews 3:1 Christ is
called the High Priest of our confession, *homologias.* It's a
word meaning to "say the same thing as," or "to agree with."
But the word Paul used in 1 Timothy 2:10 is a totally different
word, both in usage and meaning. It's a combination of *ep,*
from *epi,* meaning "to" or "upon," and the verb *angello,*
meaning "I bring a message to." The noun *angellos,* from
which the word angel comes, means "messenger."

Epaggellomai, the word Paul used, is a Greek word with two
basic meanings. It usually means "to promise, to announce that
one is about to do or furnish something."[7] In all the other
passages where it is used it means "to promise" except in 6:21
where the King James Version translates it as "profess." Arndt
and Ginrich, translators of *Bauer's Lexicon,* one of the best
and most trustworthy, said: "Profess here means to give oneself
out as an expert in something."[8] Bushnell wrote, "The verb is
often used as meaning, 'I promise,' but being in the reflexive
form, it takes a direct object after it, something is promised to
somebody."[9] She quoted Ramsay, *"Eppaggellomenais* is a
political term used to gain supporters." We're all acquainted
with that kind of flowery speech, aren't we? Politicians promise
anything in exchange for votes and support. Ramsay
explained, "This word is commonly applied to candidates in

municipal situations who announced what they intended to do for the general benefit." Therefore, women "professing godliness" (KJV) were women "promising godliness" in exchange for good works. Gnostic women, considering themselves mediators, were promising godliness if the hearer would follow their teaching. Now Paul's restriction against women teachers begins to make sense.

These deluded, deceived, untaught women, believing they possessed a special kind of hidden knowledge, taught doctrines based on myths, speculations and fables. A century or two later the Church Fathers explained these errors and named some of their leaders, including certain women. Hippolytus (third century) said, "They magnify these wretched women above the Apostles . . . so that some of them presume to assert that there is in them something superior to Christ."

One strong point of circumstantial evidence is clear. Women publicly taught while adult men listened. If this wasn't a legitimate church practice, why were they tolerated? Why did the church leaders permit them to speak at all if women couldn't teach? And if they taught before Paul gave this restriction, why stop them now? If it was once the will of God, did He change His mind? The evidence strongly implies that women taught and held church offices. Otherwise, the churches wouldn't have accepted them or given them any hearing whatsoever.

How Did Paul Answer These Gnostic Teachers?

Two perplexing problems confront those using this passage to bar women from the teaching ministry. What is the meaning of the extremely rare—it appears only once in the Scriptures—verb translated "usurp authority" in verse 12? And how does childbirth save a woman when only the blood of Christ saves?

First, Paul dealt with the Gnostic idea of mediators: "There is one God, and one mediator also between God and men, the man [*anthropos*—human] Christ Jesus" (2:5). One simple, unexplained statement of fact: Christ alone is the Mediator; therefore, there are no Gnostic mediators. Men can pray directly to God without priestly or human go-betweens. It's a marvelous statement forever settling the claim of anyone acting as a mediator between man and God. That is Christ's exclusive territory.

Next, he urged the men to pray by "lifting up holy hands." This was the customary attitude in public prayer since the dawn of history. The Psalmists urged us again and again to lift up holy hands and bless the Lord. Tertullian wrote during the second century that we pray with hands extended because then they are harmless, with head uncovered because we are not ashamed, without a prompter because we pray from the heart. Raised hands, then and now, are a sign of the surrendered will. And it's just as applicable today as Paul's other advice or commands. "Let men pray everywhere with their hands raised!"

Women Pray in the Same Manner!

Then he tells the women to pray "likewise" or in the same manner (v. 9). Most translators say something such as "Likewise, I want women to adorn themselves with proper clothing . . ." But this is questionable. How does a woman adorn herself in the same manner that men pray with raised hands? *Hosautos*, translated as "in like manner" or "likewise," refers to the previous statement. Many translators say we must supply "pray" after women. "Likewise, women pray, adorning themselves with proper clothing." How did the men pray? Then the women must pray the same way. Did the men raise their hands? Then the women must raise their hands also. *Hosautos* isn't a strange word, just difficult to obey.

Let the Women Learn!

Verse 10 addresses those women promising godliness by means of good works. This is the context of the whole passage. Were they skilled in the Word? What were the background and qualifications for their promising godliness? Paul said they were meddlers in the law, about which they knew little if anything (1:8-9). They dabbled in myths, speculation and special revelation. Hardly a proper foundation from which to teach. What was Paul's advice?

"Let a woman quietly receive instruction with entire submissiveness"! If Paul was addressing the Judaizers his stinging words would have negated the rabbinical teaching against women being educated in the law. When Paul said, "Let them learn," he was saying, "Stop keeping them ignorant, let them learn!" Regardless of whom he was instructing, his words confront the world's system head on. But he wasn't addressing Judaizers; he was addressing Gnostics. Why let *them* learn? Because their lack of pure biblical knowledge was causing confusion and their zeal had to be harnessed.

Some commentators say he spoke to individual wives since he only mentioned "a woman" and not women in general, but that argument is weak. The Greek language doesn't use an indefinite article: it is always assumed by the English translator for easier reading. Nor is there a definite article in this passage. What it says literally is "woman in silence let learn in all subjection." If this single passage prevents the wives from teaching their husbands, it frees the unmarried women from this restriction. Was Paul telling just the wives to learn, and just the wives to stop usurping their husbands' authority? Some have tried to make the apostle's words read this way by taking them out of context. In verse 9 he addressed women (*gunaikas*—plural) although he continued his advice to the woman (*gune*—singular). Nevertheles, it is the same group of women. He didn't speak to women in general in verse 9 and then isolate wives in verses 11 and 12. The women who were "promising godliness by means of good words" in verse 10 were the same women he spoke to in the following verses.

But why was he so strict with them? Learn "with entire submissiveness"! Does this mean women can't take part in the learning process? First, it should be pointed out how teaching sessions were usually conducted at that time. The popular question-and-answer format was used. Both pagan philosophers and church teachers found it effective. We know there were heated debates as ideas were tossed around and confusion piled upon confusion. We learn in 1 Timothy 1:4 and 6:20 there were endless discussions and quibbling over the meaning and interpretation of words. I'm quite convinced Paul wanted more than quiet women, he wanted submissive students of the Word, both men and women, who would learn without interruption. He wasn't suggesting total silence since he used the same word in verse 2 when he said he wanted the church to pray for governmental leaders so that we may live a tranquil and "quiet" life (1 Tim. 2:2). Whatever the word means in verse 2 it means the same thing in verse 11. Was he advocating total silence for all believers? Of course not! Quietness was a life free from arguments, stress and turmoil. What he wanted was respect for the teachers since no one can learn over the din of continual interruptions. When a session is disrupted by private conversations, "rabbit trail" side issues, and speculation until the original theme is lost, who learns anything?

The situation was desperate and demanded immediate correction, so he said in effect, "Women, sit down and learn with respect and quietness. Be reverent and learn!" He wasn't arguing for their illiteracy as the rabbis did, nor did he put them down as silly, gossipy females. He encouraged them to learn. He knew their faith wouldn't grow without a knowledge of the Word (1 Cor. 14:31; cf. Rom. 10:17). He knew that no one can teach without first being taught, so he argued, "Let them learn!"

171

Why Didn't Paul Let Women Teach?

He added in verse 12, "I do not allow a woman to teach or usurp authority over a man, but to remain quiet." We must be honest as we approach this powerful but difficult passage. If it is used correctly it can be a mighty liberating force; if it is used incorrectly it becomes a horrible binding power. As Christians we're not interested in maintaining a status quo whether it's slavery, polygamy, stoning adulterers or keeping women in their place. Over the centuries many horrible practices have been condoned by the church and the Bible used to defend them.

Was Paul saying, "I never permit a woman to teach," or "I am not now permitting a woman to teach"? The verb *ouk epitrepo* is better translated as "I am not permitting," emphasizing either the temporary nature of the answer or Paul's personal attitude.[11] Paul did not say, "I never permit a woman to teach," because he did permit it. Priscilla, his close friend and fellow disciple, taught alongside her husband! One exception breaks the rule. No one doubts that Priscilla taught. In fact, many Bible scholars believe she, and not Apollos, her husband, had the ministry in their family. Paul didn't say, "I never permit!" He said, "I am not permitting," either at this time or under certain conditions. Ephesus was one place he refused to let "a woman" teach.

What woman can't teach? Any woman? All women? Just the wives? Just the unmarried and widows? Why did Paul give Timothy this advice? To stop the Gnostic heretics from teaching? Who was this passage concerned with? Those women promising godliness by means of good works (v. 10). These women needed to sit quietly and learn (v. 11). To retain this context, his next statement remains part of his instruction. What he said, in effect, was this: "I am not permitting those unlearned, Gnostic heretics to teach." Why couldn't they teach? Because they were women?

No! Because they didn't know what they were talking about (1:3-9).

Don't Let a Woman Usurp Authority

Here's where human reasoning reaches extreme levels of assumption: concluding "usurp authority" means to usurp the man's or husband's authority. Most men won't let anyone take away their authority and leadership position unless they willingly abdicate their control. Scanzoni and Hardesty implied women were taking over the reins of church leadership, which belonged exclusively to the men.[12] It isn't possible to exercise authority over anyone unless there is first submission. In a police state, the military, or a situation where submission is enforced by jailing, death, etc., submission can be and often is enforced. However, the Christian church didn't have this kind of delegated judicial power; therefore, if a woman usurped a man's authority the man was either a passive participant or a willing partner. Once fact is obvious: if the woman usurped the church leadership, there was no male leadership.

I've researched the phrase "usurp authority" in many sources but an article by Catherine Kroeger[13] published in a scholarly evangelical paper proved to be the most enlightening. "To usurp authority" is the translation of a Greek verb, *authentein.* It's so rare that it's only found in one place in the Bible, and it was not a common word in secular usage. Why would Paul choose such an uncommon word to describe women usurping men's authority? Why did he use a rare verb that was considered vulgar and coarse? Most readers slide over this phrase without any further thought, assuming it means "authority" in the same sense the common word *exousia* is used. Christ Jesus gave power and authority *(exousia)* to overcome Satan and evil spirits (Luke 10:19), and this is the context one expects for "usurp authority" in 1 Timothy 2:12. However, the word used isn't *exousia* but *authentein. Exousia* is used thirty-two times in the New Testament and there isn't any question as to the correct meaning. It always means authority. Paul could have used this common word if the issue had been women usurping men's authority *(exousia)*, and his readers would have easily understood what he was saying. Instead he used the word *authentein*. Does this rare verb mean "to usurp authority"?

Authentein *in the Apostolic Age*

Scanzoni and Hardesty summarized their background material by saying the great Greek dramatists used it for "suicide" or a "family murderer." Later it came to mean "lord" or "autocrat." Because suicide involves deciding for oneself ... the word came to mean "self-willed" or "arbitrary," interfering in what was not properly one's own domain, trespassing beyond the socially proper limits.[14] However, Catherine Kroeger's research revealed that this strange word did not have the meaning of "to bear rule" or "usurp authority" until the third or fourth century, well after the close of the apostolic and New Testament era. Essentially the word means "to thrust oneself." Kroeger wrote, "The Attic orator Antiphon used the term *authentes* to mean 'murderer' in four different instances in legal briefs of murder cases and once to mean suicide, as did Dio Cassius. Thucydides, Herodotus, and Aeschylus also used the word to denote one who slays with his own hand, and so did Euripides. The Jewish Philo, whose writings are contemporary with the New Testament, meant 'self-murderer' by his use of the term.

"In Euripides the word begins to take on a sexual tinge. Menelaos is accounted a murderer because of his *wife's* malfeasance, and Andromache, the adored wife of the fallen Hector, is taken as a concubine by the *authentes,* who can command her domestic and sexual services. The word also occurs in a homosexual sense in a speech by Theseus, king of

Athens, where love of young boys was considered a virtue rather than a vice."[15]

More from Ms. Kroeger: "Although one finds hints in certain modern lexicons, the erotic sense of *authentes* is often ignored. The grammarian Phynichus, writing around A.D. 180, explained that the word is composed of two parts—*autos,* 'self,' and *hentos* from *hiemi;* to 'thrust out from oneself' or to 'desire.' The word should never, he announced, be used to denote tyranny, but rather murder by one's own hand, as with a sword. (The sword was considered a phallic symbol in ancient Greece.) Moeris, also in the second century, advised his students to use another word, *autodikein,* as it was less coarse than *authentein.* The Byzantine Thomas Magister reiterates the warning against using this objectional term."[16]

Kroeger's study then turned to Judaism. Pregnancy resulting from sexual orgies was common among the pagans but repugnant to the Jews. In the Septuagint Apocrypha, *Wisdom of Solomon* 12:6 mentions *authentas goneis,* "parents gendering helpless souls," in the midst of fertility and mystery rites of the Canaanites. "The crime of the *authentas* parents appears to be the procreation of souls doomed to everlasting damnation.

"In the period just before the birth of Christ *authentes* came to mean the 'author' or 'originator' of an action. Such usage occurs in Josephus, Diodorus of Sicily, Eusebius, and Polybius. By the second century A.D., the word was used for 'creator,' for a self-thrusting one could both murder and create. Most modern scholars accept the rendition of 'original status' for *authentia* in 3 Maccabees 2:29.

"In Egyptian magic and Gnostic papyri, the terms *authentes, authentikos,* and *authentia* designated the original, the primordial, the 'authentic'; and, by the third century, the concept of the primal source had merged with that of power and authority. In most ancient theologies, creative acts were

175

also sexual ones; and the erotic connotation of *authentein* lingered on.

"In a lengthy description of the various tribes' sexual habits, Michael Clycas, the Byzantine historiographer, uses this verb to describe women, 'who make sexual advances to men and fornicate as much as they please without arousing their husband's jealousy.' "[17]

How Did Paul Use Authentein?

Paul's teaching regarding women *must* be studied within the apostolic period. It was long *after* Paul wrote his epistle to Timothy that *authentein* came to mean "to exercise authority," "to bear rule over," or "to domineer." John Chrysostom (347-407) was one of the dominant Greek Church Fathers and patriarch of Constantinople. In his commentary on 1 Timothy 5:6 he used *authentia* to express "sexual license," nearly two centuries after Paul wrote Timothy. *Authentein* had not yet take on the meaning "to usurp authority."

Clement of Alexandria (d. 215), another Greek theologian, wrote several Christian defenses against Gnosticism. He argued against several groups who accepted sexual license as Christian behavior. He accused those who turned love feasts into sexual orgies, who taught women to "give to every man that asketh of thee." One such group was branded *authentia*.[18]

We know the Gnostics used sexual practices to bind the flesh and the divine together (Rev. 2:20). In most ancient pagan religions the act of procreation was a mystery; they thought fornication and in some instances homosexuality linked them to the world of the gods. Apparently, this sexual aspect of Gnosticism was incorporated with Jezebel's teaching which Jesus condemned (Rev. 3:20). The apostle Peter was aware of this problem. He mentioned the "false teachers among you . . . having eyes full of adultery and that never cease from sin . . . *accursed children* [emphasis mine] . . . and entice by fleshly desires, by sensuality, those who barely escape from the ones who live in error"(2 Pet. 2:1, 14-18). These were the same problems that plagued Ephesus where false teachers "captivate weak women weighed down with sins"(2 Tim. 3:6).

Now that we have the original meaning of *authentein,* how does it tie in with Paul's admonition? We know from verses 9-10 that women were told to "dress modestly." In a city noted for its immorality and temple prostitutes, Christian women dressed differently. Dr. Bushnell, commenting on this passage, brought out the meaning of the word *katastola* as a loose garment that reached to the feet and was worn with a girdle.[19] In other words, a spirit of self-restraint and reverence would prevent a woman from becoming a slave to fashion. Chrysostom said, "Imitate not the courtesans," when he commented on this passage.

Ephesus was famous for its shrine of Diana, where thousands of sacred prostitutes believed fornication brought believers into contact with deity in much the same way the Gnostics used *authentia* to bind the flesh and the divine together. When these women converted to Christianity they had to unlearn these pagan practices. "Virtually without exception, female teachers among the Greeks were courtesans, such as Aspasia, who numbered Socrates and Pericles among her students. Active in every major school of philosophy, these *hetairai* made it evident in the course of their lectures that they were available afterwards for a second occupation. But the Bible teaches that to seduce men in such a manner was indeed to lead them to slaughter and the halls of death (cf. Prov. 2:18; 5:5; 5:27; 9:18). The verb *authentein* is thus peculiarly apt to describe both the erotic and the murderous.'[20]

We know Paul was dealing with Gnostics, some of them female "mediators," who promised godliness in return for following them in blind obedience to their "hidden knowledge." Therefore, *authentein* must be translated as causing erotic or symbolic death, and not as usurping authority, since that meaning didn't come into usage until the third century.

With these thoughts in mind, we conclude that what Paul argued was this:

1. Gnostic "mediators" were sharing their "hidden knowledge" based on fables and superstitions. Paul said, there is one mediator between God and men, the man Christ Jesus.

2. Gnostic teachers promised a form of godliness that can be achieved by means of good works. Paul said, "Let a woman quietly receive instruction with entire submissiveness."

3. Those Gnostics enticed their male students with sexual overtures. Paul thundered that he would not permit a woman to teach men by using female wiles.

4. Gnostics believed Eve was created first, then Adam. Paul said, "It was Adam who was first created, and then Eve."

5. Gnostics taught that Eve received secret knowledge when she ate from the forbidden tree; therefore, female teachers could give that knowledge. Paul countered by saying Eve was deceived, but Adam was not deceived. Rather than the woman receiving knowledge, she was blinded and fell into sin; she received death, not "secret wisdom."

Blame It On Adam!

Verses 13 and 14 are Paul's facts for not allowing these women the teaching ministry. "For it was Adam who was first created, and then Eve. And it was not Adam who was deceived, but the woman being quite deceived, fell into transgression." How could the woman stand in an exalted position when she was thoroughly deceived and made after the man? Her "hidden knowledge" wasn't truth but deception. The words "quite deceived" have the meaning of complete deception. Eve was so unaware she had been victimized as to believe she was taking the proper action. When a person is completely deceived, even their wrong actions seem right.

These two verses are directly linked to verse 12 by the word "for" or "because." The statement in verse 12 is based on the facts of verses 13 and 14. How could Eve have special knowledge as Adam's lifegiver when he was created first? That's why Paul stressed the traditional interpretation that Adam wasn't tempted or deceived. Adam wasn't taken in by the serpent's persuasion; he acted on his own. Yet Eve was beguiled into believing the lie, and fell into the transgression. Therefore, Paul argued, how could she be revered as the one who enlightened humanity? In two short statements, he pulled down the stronghold of Gnosticism. With one statement of eternal fact he yanked them from their role as mediators. With one point of logic he nullified the claim to secret knowledge. How could Eve have had a special *gnosis* when she was deceived?

A Word of Caution and Balance

We must be careful to stop here and not carry Paul's argument beyond his intended purpose. Did Paul use the creation order and Eve's deception to refute and defuse the Gnostic women in Ephesus, but also to forbid all women for all time from public teaching when males are present? It's important the church doesn't put people in bondage based on improper or incomplete exegesis. Any teaching that could destroy any Spirit-anointed, Spirit-appointed ministry must be clearly understood.

Paul was thoroughly versed in the Jewish theology that labeled women inferior and considered them property rather than persons. He understood the traditions binding these women and he knew that all the traditions were rooted in the creation order and the Fall, facts he reiterated in verses 13 and 14. Was this his final statement?

Is Woman Saved By Having Babies?

> But women shall be preserved through the bearing
> of children if they continue in faith and love and
> sanctity with self restraint (v. 15).

Here is another difficult and confusing passage. Even the
translations don't agree. The New American Standard Bible
says, "But women . . ." The Greek text says, "But she shall be
saved." The problem is is Paul's shift from the singular
pronoun "she" to the plural "they" in the same sentence. Paul's
term "a woman" in verse 12 becomes "she" in verse 15 and
"they" in the last phrase. This statement is his conclusion to the
Gnostic women question.

Was Paul saying women will be saved by bearing children?
The verb tense is future while salvation from sin is a finished
work. Talmudic Judaism said yes. "Whereby do women earn
merit? By making their children go to synagogue to learn
scripture and their husbands to Beth Hamidrash to learn
Mishnah, and waiting for their husband's return."[21] The
section in the Babylonian Talmud, Sotah 21a, says almost the
same thing: a woman gains (earns her salvation) by sending her
sons and husband to study the law. Judaism has never taught
salvation by grace through faith but rather by good works
(Rom. 4). But Paul wasn't talking to Judaizers but Gnostics.

Does this verse mean women can earn their salvation
through childbirth apart from the blood of Christ? His epistle
to this church stressed salvation by grace through faith, not by
works. This thesis is excluded (Eph. 2:8-10), since it violently
contradicts Paul's inspired teaching. Neither does it account
for his shift from the singular to the plural in the same
statement.

Some teachers have suggested this verse means "saved by the
birth of the child Christ Jesus" because of the Greek definite
article. But this overlooks the statement "She shall be saved by

the birth of the child." All believers accept the blessed truth that Jesus was "born of a woman"(Gal. 4:4), "in the likeness of men"(Phil. 2:7). However, the emphasis is not on salvation but deity being made flesh in order to redeem mankind. No one is saved by the birth of the Christ child but by His death and resurrection. If Paul's statement in 1 Timothy 2:15 is understood in this light it makes the incarnation the means of our salvation, again inconsistent with the Pauline revelation. There is one other idea. The mother will be saved through the dangers of childbirth if "they continue in faith." This is true but completely out of context. Paul wasn't talking about the dangers of birth but Gnostic heretics.

She Shall Be Saved!

There is one final possibility. Verse 15 begins with "but" linking it to the two previous verses which are also linked to the troublesome verse 12, constituting one complete thought. "But she shall be saved." Who is the singular she? There is only one mentioned, Eve, who was made after Adam, and it was she who sinned.

Paul's stand against the Gnostic women teaching and *authentein* appears to be a temporary injunction in verse 12 but seems to become permanent in verses 13 and 14 based on the creation order and Eve's deception. He used these basic, beginning events to counter and overturn the Gnostic heresy that glorified Eve as the bringer of both knowledge and life to man. By emphasizing the fact that Adam was not deceived by the serpent's *gnosis* but that Eve was, Paul denied Eve to be the one who enlightened humanity. His orthodox argument apparently solved the Ephesian problem. However, he knew the Genesis events had and were being used to silence women in church. Whether he used them as illustrations or principles is unknown to us. What is obvious to us is he didn't end his teaching here.

He knew the two Genesis accounts kept women bound to a theological position that prohibited full function in Christ's body, so he continued with "But she shall be saved." He also knew that until those traditions and conditions were canceled or changed, the bondage would remain. She shall be saved from what? Was not Paul saying women shall be saved from the conditions outlined in verses 13 and 14? Saved from the hierarchal order of creation, saved from the results of Eve's deception, saved into spiritual and social wholeness!

The aspect of childbearing was briefly mentioned when we discussed 1 Corinthians 11:8-9, which is a parallel argument. Paul presented his case, based on the creation order, against men wearing a covering and allowing women to continue wearing theirs. Man does not come from the woman, but woman from the man and woman was made for the man (1 Cor. 11:8-9). Paul didn't leave his argument there but showed another side. "However, in the Lord," neither is woman independent of man, nor is man independent of woman. For as the woman originates from the man, so also the man has his birth through the woman; and all things originate from God. In the Lord there is a mutual dependency. The order of creation, which made man the source of the woman's life, is counterbalanced by the natural order of man's birth. Since the birth of the first child, man has had his origin in woman, and, Paul adds, all things originate in God. The one balances the other. Man's preeminence over woman in creation is balanced by the preeminence of woman in childbearing.

If there was a hierarchy based on the male-female order of creation it wasn't a permanent one, since woman became the origin of man. If there were a hierarchy based on the creation order, there would also be a hierarchy based on the natural order of childbirth once woman gave birth to a male. But Paul continually taught against hierarchies. Whether he taught on the male-female relationship or the marriage order, mutual dependence was always his theme. In the church he taught against the head thinking it is better than or assuming authority over the foot (1 Cor. 12:20-23). Mutual dependence is also his counterbalance to the male hierarchy supposedly based on creation. If there was a subservient role because the woman was made after the man, childbirth canceled it.

In verse 13 he recognized the ramifications of the woman's fall and transgression. The "she" who shall be saved is singular since Paul was speaking about Eve. How would childbearing overcome the fact that she was deceived? Genesis 3:15 is one of the most important covenant promises in Scripture. "I will put enmity Between you and the woman, And between your seed and her seed . . ." The promise to deliver humanity was directly linked to the seed of the woman, the fruit of her childbearing. Satan deceived Eve; her "child" would defeat Satan. In this context, "the bearing of the child" could refer to the birth of Christ. However, this isn't the way a woman earns her salvation from sin and death. Rather, through her giving birth, Christ, the seed of the woman would come, and He would destroy all the works of the devil (1 John 3:8). He would fulfill the prophetic curse made by God. He would become a curse for us in order to redeem us from the curse of the law (Gal. 3:13). A woman is saved through the blood of Christ just as a man is. Woman shall be saved from the results of the deception and transgression of Eve. Therefore, childbearing counterbalanced the creation order that made man preeminent, and eliminated the consequences of her deception. Womankind is free from all the effects of the Creation order and the Fall. Christ marked the bill, "Paid in Full"!

Paul systematically clarified each point of his argument except the "they" in verse 15. The "she" is Eve, the subject of verses 13 and 14. Woman shall be restored to her former glory as before the Fall because woman bears children, but women, "they" in verse 15, must walk in faith, love and reverence.

Just bearing children doesn't qualify a woman for restoration. Every step we take in God is a step of faith. Individual women shall be restored if they walk in faith. It isn't necessary that they bear children themselves since Eve bore *the* child and as women they share the benefits. But they must manifest the faith walk. These women had mixed biblical truth with Gnostic fables; they had ceased walking in faith. Paul didn't tell them to stop teaching because they were women but because they were in error and out of faith. These women, "they" in verse 15, may be restored, they may be delivered, they may be saved, and allowed to teach as they continue in faith and love and sanctify themselves with self-restraint.

Summing up what has been stated, a paraphrase of this passage might read:

"Let a woman quietly learn, without interruptions and questions. Presently I'm not permitting a woman to teach anyone or exercise her sexual wiles to control a man, but to be reverent and peaceful. Because Adam was formed first, and then Eve. And it wasn't Adam who was deceived—Eve was thoroughly deceived and became a transgressor.

"Nevertheless, woman shall be delivered from the condition that requires her silence; she will some day be restored and able to teach. This is possible because childbearing, by producing the seed who destroyed Satan's power, balances the superior position of man established in the creation order. However, women can only be restored as they walk in faith and love."

It is tragic that women called and anointed by God are kept from their ministries by the use of 1 Timothy 2:12. The primary purpose for the baptism in the Holy Spirit is power for ministry (Acts 1:8). Why would God baptize the women, including the mother of Jesus, in the Holy Spirit and then forbid them to exercise the indwelling Spirit's ministry? Any idea that God could not or would not speak through a woman simply because she is female contradicts the whole New Testament teaching of Jesus Christ and the apostle Paul. No person, male or female, is called by God on the basis of sex, but on the basis of commitment to Him. In Christ there is neither male nor female.

Chapter Sixteen Notes

1. Susan Foh, *Women and the Word of God* (Phillipsburg, NJ: Presbyterian and Reformed Publishing Co., 1979), pp. 247-248.

2. Ibid.

3. W.E. Vine, *Expository Dictionary of New Testament Words* (Old Tappan, NJ: Fleming H. Revell, 1966), p. 34.

4. "1 Timothy," *The Pulpit Commentary* (Grand Rapids, MI: Eerdmans, 1950), p. 2.

5. See 1 Timothy 1:3-11; 4:1-10; 5:11-15; 6:3-4; 2 Timothy 1:15; 2:14-18; 3:1-9; 3:13; 4:3-4; Titus 1:10-16; 3:9-11.

6. Susan Foh, op. cit., p. 122.

7. Joseph Thayer, *Greek-English Lexicon of the New Testament* (Grand Rapids, MI: Zondervan, 1968), p. 277.

8. Bauer, Arndt, & Ginrich, *A Greek-English Lexicon of the New Testament* (Chicago: University of Chicago Press, 1958), p. 280.

9. Katherine Bushnell, *God's Word to Women*, (1923, privately reprinted by Ray Munson, N. Collins, NY), p. 331.

10. Ibid., p. 332.

11. Don Williams, *The Apostle Paul and Women in the Church* (Ventura, CA: Regal Books, 1977), p. 112.

12. Letha Scanzoni & Nancy Hardesty, *All We're Meant To Be* (Waco, TX: Word Books, 1974), p. 71.

13. Catherine Kroeger, "Ancient Heresies and a Strange Greek Verb," *The Reformed Journal*, March 1979.

14. Letha Scanzoni & Nancy Hardesty, op. cit., p. 71.

15. Catherine Kroeger, op. cit., p. 13.

16. Ibid.

17. Ibid.

18. Ibid.

19. Katherine Bushnell, op. cit., p. 330.

20. Catherine Kroeger, op. cit., p. 14.

21. Babylonain Talmud, Berahoth, 17a.

17

Paul, Women and the Ministry

Even though this chapter concentrates on women in Christian ministry, we won't relate how Jesus treated women except to say He went against the Jewish traditions. Whether it was His deep concern for the ageless oppression of widows, His praise for the widow's mite in the temple offering, or touching the unclean woman, He uplifted and enhanced their dignity. They traveled with Him, talked publicly with Him, and followed Him as His disciples. He adjusted the unjust balances working against them by forgiving the adulterous woman and pointing His righteous finger at the equally guilty men who kept a double standard. It would be an exciting and rewarding study to explore the number of Jewish taboos He violated during His earthly ministry. But this study is confined mainly to the attitudes of the apostle Paul, who has been charged with being misogynist.

Women Active in the New Testament
On Pentecost, there were women who received the baptism in the Holy Spirit accompanied by the same charismatic anointing and power as the men (Acts 1:14). Both sexes spoke

publicly with tongues and prophesied (Acts 2:1-4). Many of the first converts were women (Acts 5:14), who were persecuted by Paul (Acts 8:3; 9:1-2). Lydia was possbily the first and most notable European convert (Acts 16:14). Scripture tells us many of these women were not from the common stratum of society since "a number of the leading women" were converts (Acts 17:4).

Women Who Worked With Paul

Before his conversion on the Damascus road, Saul (Paul's given name) was an active rabbinical student doing his fanatical best to stamp out the new sect of Christians (Acts 8:3; 9:1-2; 22:4-5). His qualifications, listed in Philippians 3:1-6, show he was more than the average worshiper; he was determined to promote his faith. Then he met Christ Jesus and his life changed. Henceforth called Paul, he preached Jesus Christ to both men and women. He mentioned several of those women by name in his letter to the Romans.

There was Phoebe, a *deacon* of the church in Cenchrea (16:1), and Priscilla, whom he called "my fellow-worker" (16:3). Both Priscilla and Aquila enjoyed equal standing— Paul accepted them as associates, and not just followers. He also mentioned four other women: Mary, Tryphaena, Tryphosa and Persis, all active, hard-working gospel laborers. Summing it up, he closed this epistle by greeting twenty-eight different persons, ten of them women. Just naming them shocks some traditionalists who say Paul silenced women and denied them any place in public ministry. He mentioned Junia as a fellow worker who was "outstanding among the apostles" (16:7). The suggestion that Junia could be Junias (masculine) will be answered later in this study.

Finally, in his Philippian letter, he urged Euodia and Syntyche to quit their fussing and settle their differences while at the same time commending them for struggling with him in the ministry. He used the verb, *sunethlesan,* a combative term used of athletics. Apparently these two women supplied more than just moral and spiritual support; they were in the center ring with Paul.

Some of the women believers were called "leaders" in the church. Many scholars believe that Chloe, the woman who reported the problems at Corinth to Paul, was a house church leader. House churches met in private homes during the early years of the church. Luke, the historian, mentioned the first house church. Peter went straight "to the house of Mary, the mother of John who was also called Mark," Mark being the author of the gospel bearing his name. Mark's father isn't mentioned nor is any other male worker. If a man was the leader, why didn't Luke mention him? Apparently Mark's mother was the elder or church leader in her home (Acts 12:12).

A more conclusive example is Lydia, Paul's first Philippian convert. No one questions that the church met in her home (Acts 16:14-15, 40). If she had a husband, he isn't mentioned in the Scriptures. It was the ordinary practice to meet in the home of the presiding elder. It doesn't seem likely the church would have met in one home if the church leader lived somewhere else. The modern practice of hiring a pastor, preacher or priest was unheard of, and all elders were chosen from within the local church body. When Paul left Ephesus, he appointed and ordained elders from among the spiritually mature believers to oversee the flock and guard it from the spiritual wolves who would soon invade it. We can't insist that Lydia was the leading elder, but if her local church followed the common pattern, she was an elder.

Nympha of Laodicea led the church which met in her house (Col. 4:15). Her situation falls into the same category as Lydia but there is a plus in favor of her being the house church leader. Whenever Paul mentioned a church leader he specifically named the person in charge. This is verified in Philemon 1:2

where Archippus, his fellow soldier, also conducted a church in his house, assisted by Apphia, a woman. Finally, there is the best-known woman Bible teacher in the New Testament, Priscilla. She, along with her husband, conducted a church in their house (1 Cor. 16:19). Although the accepted way of addressing a husband and wife was to mention the husband's name first, Paul reversed this order, giving basis to the idea that the wife was the real teacher in the family (Rom. 16:3; 2 Tim. 4:19; cf. Acts 18:18, 26). When the church met in a female's home it was "her" house, but when it met in the home of a male leader it was "his" house, or in the case of Priscilla and Aquila, a team, it was "their" house.

Women as Apostles

There isn't much said about women apostles but one is specifically mentioned. In Romans 16:6-8, Paul mentioned Junia, an outstanding apostle and fellow prisoner. It is argued that Junia could be Junias, a man's name, but scholars aren't absolutely sure which gender is meant, since both the names Andronikos and Junian are in the accusative case. Rather than beginning from a base of uncertainty, it is possible to search the writings of the early church fathers who were much closer to the original manuscripts and church than we are today.

John Chrysostom (337-407), bishop of Constantinople, wasn't partial to women. He said some negative things about women but spoke positively about Junia. "Oh, how great is the devotion of this woman that she should be counted worthy of the appellation of apostle!"[1] Nor was he the only church father to believe Junia was a woman. Origen of Alexandria (c. 185-253) said the name was a variant of Julia (Rom. 16:15), as does *Thayer's Lexicon.*[2] Leonard Swidler cited Jerome (340-419), Hatto of Vercelli (924-961), Theophylack (1050-1108), and Peter Abelard (1079-1142) as believing Junia to be a woman.

Dr. Swidler stated, "To the best of my knowledge, no commentator on the text until Aegidus of Rome (1245-1316) took the name to be masculine."[3] Apparently the idea that Junia was a man's name is a relatively modern concept but the bulk of the best evidence available is that Junia was indeed a woman, and an outstanding apostle. What would Junia have been doing in prison with Paul if she was a confined, quiet lady? Surely, a silent woman wouldn't have generated enough evidence to convict her of being a Christian!

A common counter-argument against any woman being an apostle is this: Why didn't Jesus choose at least one woman among His apostles? Christ ministered primarily to the house of Israel (Matt. 15:24). He preached to Jews who were governed by both the Bible and the oral law. Jesus knew the oral law forbade women witnesses in both civil and religious matters. "The law about an oath of testimony applies to men but not to women."[4] One of those curses supposedly placed on women because of Eve's transgression says, "She is not to be believed as a witness."[5]

Christ chose His apostles for one main purpose, to bear witness of His resurrection (Acts 1:21-22). One of the requirements for being an apostle was being with Him through the time of His death and resurrection. They lived together as a family. It would have been highly questionable, or wrong ethically, morally, and culturally, for a woman to be part of that original group. No Jew would have accepted her witness.

But Junia wasn't one of the twelve apostles; she was a New Testament church apostle, as was Paul. Ephesians 4:8-11 tells us these apostles were not ordained until after Jesus ascended, and their qualifications were vastly different than those governing the twelve. Only one of the original twelve was ever replaced. Matthias took Judas's place. After that time no living person could fulfill the necessary requirements (Acts 1:21-22). Paul wasn't considered one of the twelve and frequently argued the validity of his apostleship. Junia could have been one of the New Testament church apostles, although not one of Jesus' original apostles.

Women as Prophets

If there is any doubt about Junia being an apostle, there isn't any question about women prophets called and anointed by God, since both testaments mention several.

When Mary and Joseph brought the baby Jesus to the temple for circumcision they were met by Anna the prophetess who served God daily in the Temple. The Scriptures make no distinction between "a prophet" and "a prophetess" except that one is masculine and the other feminine. Obviously, there weren't as many women prophets as there were male; nevertheless, they both served God in the prophetic office. Anna ministered as a Hebrew prophet during the last days of the Old Covenant and during the beginning of the new as one who ministered to the Lord Jesus Christ (Luke 2:36-38).

There was Elizabeth, the mother of the Baptist. Luke 1:41-45 says she was "filled with the Holy Spirit" and spoke the word of God. Certainly, Mary's Magnificat is a marvelous portion of the Word of God. Included among the women prophets were those who spoke on the day of Pentecost, including Mary, our Lord's mother. They all spoke in tongues and magnified the Lord (Acts 2:4).

Later, when Peter explained to the amazed Jews what has happened, he quoted Joel: "In the last days . . . your daughters shall prophesy . . . even My bondslaves, both men and women" (Acts 2:17-18). God said women can and should prophesy (1 Cor. 11:3-5). If prophecy is predicting, they can predict. If it is proclaiming, they can proclaim. If it is correcting, they can correct. If it is teaching, they can teach. If it is preaching, they can preach. Whatever prophecy is for men, it is the same for women. It isn't gender that makes one prophesy but the anointing of the Spirit.

Philip had four daughters who prophesied (Acts 21:9), virgin sisters who guided the apostle Paul by warning and instructing him through their ministry gift. It's interesting to note that Paul only stayed with the brethren at Ptolemais one day but spent several days with Philip's daughters. The lasting influence of these women prophets was so powerfully and generally accepted in the early church that their burial place was used to verify certain claims of apostolicity in a dispute with the Bishop Polycrates against Pope Victor I.[6]

Although she was undoubtedly a Gnostic, Jezebel's prophetic influence was accepted by the church at Thyatira (Rev. 2:20-23). Her erroneous ideas on immorality and about eating food offered to idols, one of the four restrictions binding on gentile believers (Acts 15:18-29), were accepted by the church leaders. She not only taught *(didaskein)* through her prophecy, she was encouraged *(aphesis)* by the local church. Regardless of her evil ways, which is not the issue here, her prophetic influence was accepted. If women weren't supposed to teach men, this would have been the best place for the Lord to make it known. Jesus could have rebuked her, silenced her, and put an end to women's teaching. Instead, He gave her opportunity to repent, not of teaching, but of her immorality and error. An interesting note is that Thyatira later became the place where the Montanists, a second-century cult, flourished. Women prophets were an important part of Montanism.

Women as Teachers

Foremost among the women teachers was Priscilla, apparently the teacher of the Priscilla and Aquila team. They are mentioned six times in separate scriptural accounts. The fact that she, along with her husband, taught the eloquent preacher Apollos reveals the prominent place women had in primitive Christianity.

When Paul first met this amazing couple, he addressed them as Aquila and Priscilla (Acts 18:2), the normal way of addressing couples, with the prominent person, usually the husband, named first. But after listening to this team minister he put her first. John Chrysostom said, "He did not do so without reason: the wife must have had, I think, greater piety than her husband. This is not simple conjecture; its confirmation is evident in the Acts."[7]

Was she teaching foundational truths? What was the "more excellent way" she expounded to Apollos? The development of deep truth and heavy doctrine was still centuries away. At this stage of the church's growth she must have been teaching the full gospel. Most scholars agree there were women teachers—evidence is abundantly clear and impossible to explain away.

Women as Deacons

In the beginning there were no servants called "deaconesses," only "deacons." The word *diakonos* occurs thirty times and it is usually translated "minister." Seven times the King James Version renders it "servant," and three times "deacon." The feminine noun "deaconess" wasn't used until the third century, which places it well outside New Testament studies. For the first 250 years, the ministers, men or women, were called deacons.

Phoebe was a deacon (Rom. 16:1), whom Paul called a "ruler" (prostatis) of many (Rom 16:2). The King James Version used the word "succourer" but the word *prostatis* isn't translated that way anywhere else in the Greek Scriptures It was a common, classical word meaning "patroness or protectoress, a woman set over others."[8'9] It's the feminine form of the masculine noun *prostates,* which means "defender" or "guardian" when it refers to men. In 1 Timothy 3:4-5, 12 and

5:17, the verb *proistemi* is used of the qualifications for bishops and deacons when Paul charged the men to "rule" well their households, which included caring for their needs. Whatever it means for men, it must mean the same for women. Whatever these bishops and deacons did for their households, Phoebe did for the church and Paul. The positions were identical.

If we refuse to admit that Phoebe "ruled," or "led" or was a "defender" or "guardian" then we must reduce the male deacons to whatever level Phoebe was ministering. If Phoebe just "succoured," then that's all the male deacons did. It's quite inconsistent to translate the word as "ruler" when it refers to men and "succourer" when it refers to women.

Women deacons were ordained just as the men were ordained and history records the changing status of women as the apostolic age closed. (More of this vital statement later.) Paul gave both Timothy and Titus guidelines for choosing candidates for the ministries of bishop and deacon. Most scholars agree that in the original church there were no differences between *episkopos* (bishop) and *presbuteros* (presbyter or elder). Both words describe the same office. The biblical title "bishop" had little if anything in common with modern denominational church bishops with translocal authority.

The word *hosautos,* translated "likewise" or "in manner," included women as candidates (1 Tim. 3:11). Paul first outlined the requirements for bishops and deacons. Then he continued, "Likewise [*hosautos*], women," and included their qualifications. *Hosautos* definitely links the two subjects together. First the qualifications for men who desire the office of bishop and then the added requirements for women who desire same ministry. Some commentators say Paul gave additional requirements for the bishops' and deacons' wives. Since there isn't a definite article in the sentence construction, nor is the possessive case used, this suggestion must be rejected.

Further, Paul's opening statement is wide open to both sexes. "This is a true saying, If a man [*tis*] desire the office . . ." *Tis* is a neuter word meaning either male or female, someone or a certain one, usually meaning both sexes. If the Holy Spirit wanted only males for these church offices, Paul would have used *aner,* the unmistakable word for man.

Does church history affirm the place of women deacons? Records reveal that the Eastern Church continued ordaining women deacons into the fourth century while the Western Church continued well into the second century. *The Ante-Nicene Fathers* records the Apostolic Constitutions in which bishops were charged to ordain women deacons. "Ordain also a woman deacon who is faithful and holy."[10] The Council of Nicea in 325, numbered women deacons among the clergy.[11] The Council of Chalcedon in 451 listed the requirements for ordaining women deacons.[12] Even earlier, the non-Christian historian Pliny the Younger, a Roman orator, naturalist and statesman, wrote a letter about his research among Christians to the Emperor Trajan, who reigned from A.D. 98 to 117: "I judged it so much the more necessary to extract the real truth with the assistance of torture, from two maidservants, who were called deacons: but I could discover nothing more than the depraved and excessive superstition."[13]

During the second century, as apostasy set in, women's ministries began changing, especially in the Western Church. Several statements gleaned from the Apostolic Constitutions, when linked together, describe the deterioration. An early third-century writing called the *Didascalia* (teaching) said that persons being baptized came up from the water and were received and taught by the woman deacons, so such women were still teaching during the third century.[14] However, by this period they were being called deaconesses rather than deacons. Their ministries were considered lesser than those of the male deacons, yet they were still ordained and called clerics.

By the time the Council of Orange convened in 441, the change was nearly complete. The Council directed, "Let no one proceed to the ordination of deaconesses anymore."[15] Seventy-five years later, the Council of Epaon decreed in Canon 21, "We abrogate completely in the entire kingdom the consecration of widows who are named deaconesses." Sixteen years later the Council of Orleans took the church all the way back to the traditions of the Jewish elders: "No longer shall the blessing of women deaconesses be given, because of the weakness of the sex."[16]

During the Apostolic Age, women were deacons, just as men were (Rom. 16:1-2; 1 Tim. 3:12), but by the late fourth century women deacons were being called deaconesses, a new term not found in the Scriptures, and were subordinate to male deacons, even though they were still ordained as clerics. By the twelfth century, in both the Eastern and Western Church, the order of deaconesses had almost disappeared.[17]

For the first 500 years there was no mention of the weakness of women. It took the church all this time to discover they were unqualified to be deacons. Once again the spirit of the Judaizers was alive in Christ's church. The rabbinical traditions and human assumptions were not only accepted by the church leaders, they were being taught as truth. Women were considered too weak to minister even though Paul said that in Christ there is neither male nor female. Yet this attitude shouldn't amaze the reader since by this time in church history the doctrinal, moral and spiritual apostasy was nearly complete and many practices of the church were foreign to the Scriptures.

Women as Presbyters

Were there women elders or presbyters? We know Paul ordained elders and left them in charge of the church at Ephesus. If women were included in this group, they came under the same qualifications Paul gave to Timothy, the youthful bishop at Ephesus.

After completing his list of qualifications for bishops and deacons (1 Tim. 3:1-10), he continued by including the women when he said, *"gunaikas hosautos"* or "women likewise."

Hosautos links the entire list of qualifications into one single theme. It links the deacons with the bishops in verse 8 and then links them to women in verse 11. In 1 Timothy 4 and 5:17-19 Paul discussed the office of the presbyter (elder). The usual translation is "older men" and "older women," but the Greek word is the same one used for elders elsewhere. If consistency is to be maintained, then *presbutero* and *presbuteras* should be translated as men presbyters and women presbyters. A more nearly correct translation would be, "Do not sharply rebuke a male presbyter, but appeal to him as a father, to the young men as brothers, women presbyters as mothers, and the younger women as sisters, in all purity."

Thayer's Lexicon defines *presbuteros, -a, -ou,* as "a term of rank or office . . . because in early times the rulers of the people, judges, etc., were selected from the elderly men . . . among Christians, those who presided over the assemblies (or churches) . . . they did not differ at all from the *(episkopoi)* bishops or overseers (as is acknowledged also by Jerome in Titus 1:5). . . . The title *episkopos* denotes the function, *presbuteros* the dignity; the former was borrowed from Greek institutions, the latter from the Jewish."[18]

Were There Women Officers in the Church?

Most scholars agree the term "elect lady" in 2 John was not a symbol of a church, but the "overseer" of a church. Later church history used "elect persons" as a designation for church officers. Clement of Alexandria in the second century used this term when addressing church authorities, underscoring the idea that the "elect lady" was a woman church officer.[19]

From the evidence we have seen, we may conclude that women functioned as apostles, prophets, evangelists, teachers, and pastors as well as presbyters and deacons. The original church, breathed into existence by the Spirit of God, knew no distinctions between male and female ministries in Christ.

Chapter Seventeen Notes

1. *The Homilies of St. John Chrysostom, Nicene and Post-Nicene Fathers, Series I* (Grand Rapids, MI: Eerdmans, 1956).
2. Joseph Thayer, *Greek-English Lexicon of the New Testament* (Grand Rapids, MI: Zondervan, 1968), p. 306.
3. Leonard Swidler, *Biblical Affirmations of Women* (Philadelphia, PA: Westminster Press, 1979), p. 299.
4. *Shab.* 4, 1: *Sifre Dt.* 190.
5. *Midrash Pirke Rel* 14, 7d, 7.
6. *Ecclesiastical History of Eusebius* 111.31.
7. Leonard Swidler, op. cit., p. 298.
8. Joseph Thayer, op. cit., p. 549.
9. Bauer, Arndt & Ginrich, *A Greek-English Lexicon of the New Testament* (Chicago: University of Chicago Press, 1958), p. 726.
10. *The Ante-Nicene Fathers* (Grand Rapids, MI: Eerdmans, 1979), Vol. 7, p. 431.
11. Ibid., Vol. 2, p. 676.
12. Ibid., Vol. 7, p. 364.
13. Leonard Swidler, op. cit., p. 313.
14. Ibid.
15. Ibid., p. 314.
16. Ibid.
17. Ibid., p. 315.
18. Joseph Thayer, op. cit., pp. 535-36.
19. Leonard Swidler, op. cit., p. 316.

18

Women Ministers
and the Church Fathers

The period between A.D. 100 and 1000 is known as the Patristic Period from *pater,* Latin for "fathers." It lasted until Anselm of Canterbury initiated the Scholastic Period. The Greek and Latin Fathers, along with the rulings of the first seven church councils, did for Christianity what rabbinicism did for Judaism. Many of them were outspokenly negative toward women and worked to exclude them from all church service. It's unfortunate many current leaders quote these Fathers as their source and authority for silencing women in the church.

The historical evidence shows women exercised strong leadership roles through the third century. The following brief overview will point out the direction the church took, the developing attitudes, and the reasons why women were barred from public ministry. The following statements are from Fathers in both the Greek and Latin churches.

Clement of Alexandria (150-215)
Clement headed the Catechetical School of Alexandria, Egypt. His writings reveal a magnificent intelligence and

reasoning ability, but he apparently had a problem with his masculinity. "Man is stronger," he wrote, "and purer since he is uncastrated and has a beard. Women are weak, passive, castrated and immature . . . His beard, then, is the badge of a man and shows him unmistakably to be a man. It is older than Eve and is a symbol of the stronger nature. By God's decree, hairiness is one of man's conspicuous qualities, and, at that, is distributed over his whole body. For what is hairy is by nature drier and warmer than what is bare; therefore, the male is hairer and more warm-blooded than the female; the uncastrated, than the castrated; the mature, than the immature."[1]

Clement was undoubtedly honest, although partial toward men. It is said he allowed women into his lectures and spoke of their equality of nature, but more often than not he extolled man's masculinity, maturity and beard. In today's society he would be branded not a Church Father but prejudiced, ignorant and chauvinistic since hair has absolutely nothing to do with strength. Hormones make the difference. If hairiness symbolizes masculine superiority and strength, Oriental, American Indian and Scandinavian men must be weaker and inferior since they are notably less hairy than European and Latin men. Was he speaking of emotional warmth? Women tend to have outgoing personalities while most men are comparatively withdrawn. Clement may have been an intellectual giant but his attitude toward women was prejudicial, not factual. His conclusions must be rejected as erroneous.

Origen (135-245)

As one of Clement's personal students, Origen succeeded him as head of the school at Alexandria. Like his teacher, he was a strong leader, but radical in some areas.

Gnosticism is diametrically opposed to Christianity, yet it

influenced Origen's Christian thought. As a young man
he chose to live an ascetic life involving fasting, denying himself
sleep, walking barefoot, and living in poverty. Like the
Gnostics, he accepted celibacy as the purifying power that
would release him from what he believed was the fallen state.
History says he took Matthew 19:12 literally and castrated
himself.[2] He argued that God would never stoop to look on
anything feminine, forgetting that the Almighty chose a virgin
in whom to plant the seed of the Messiah. He forgot that Jesus
baptized both men and women in the Spirit at Pentecost.

His writings hint of his prejudiced theology and bent toward
the ancient rabbis. "It is not proper for a woman to speak
in church, however admirable or holy what she says may be,
merely because it comes from female lips."[3] The Gnostic
influence on his thinking prompted his teaching that the Spirit
was pure, separated and divine while the flesh was evil, earthly
and sensual. To Origen, all women were the opposite of spirit;
therefore, they were earthly, fleshly and evil.

Nor was he the only Father who embraced the rabbinical
teachings Jesus renounced. Bishop Dionysius (190-264)
followed Origen as the headmaster of the school. It
seems several of Alexandria's bishops had a faculty for
introducing error. Most famous was Arius (256-336), who
developed the heretical Godhead doctrine known as Arianism,
now taught by Jehovah's Witnesses. Dionysius re-introduced
the rabbinical teachings about female impurities by refusing
women entrance to the church building during their menstrual
period.[4]

Later, Epiphanius (315-403) claimed that the "female was
easily seduced, weak, and void of understanding. Masculine
reasoning will destroy this female folly."[5]

Even though John Chrysostom (347-407) admired Junia, the
woman apostle, he was generally negative toward women. He
called women "whitewashed tombstones," saying that inside

they are full of filth, and that marriage was given to men to keep them from submitting to prostitutes.[6]

According to Dr. Bushnell, "Woman's only century, in the Christian Church, was during the apostolic days, and a little while thereafter. Professor Ramsay, in his valuable book, *The Church in the Roman Empire,* states: 'The Universal and Catholic type of Christianity became confirmed in its dislike of the prominence and the public ministration of women. the dislike became abhorrence.' "[7]

Tertullian (160-225)

Another North African, he was the first Latin Father and a prolific, polemical writer whose works are second only to those of Augustine. During his early life he was a lawyer, thoroughly trained in Roman law. Apparently an argumentive approach in both style and thought soon placed him outside the Catholic Church. According to Jerome, Tertullian renounced his priesthood around 212 and joined the Montanists, one of the first hyper-charismatic cults, and considered heretical by the Catholic Church. Montanus believed he was chosen to restore the church to its original simplicity with the full use of spiritual gifts. This movement expanded rapidly during the second century, exposing the loss of spiritual power in the established church. The Montanists discouraged marriage, and advised continence for those already married. Eusebius, the famed church historian, described the Montanists as "poisonous reptiles, crawling over Asia and Phrygia."

Tertullian eventually left the movement, but, unfortunately, his Montanist ideas toward woman and marriage continued to influence his thinking. Many of his lectures were anti-woman. He saw woman as a personification of fundamentally evil sex and men as the innocent victims of feminine wiles. He too believed man to be stronger because he has a beard and was created first. Like the rabbis, he blamed Eve for bringing sin and death into the world, but he also blamed woman for the death of the Son of God: "You are the devil's gateway, you are the unsealer of that [forbidden] tree; you are the first deserter of the divine law; you are she who persuaded him whom the devil was not valiant enough to attack. You destroyed so easily God's image, man."[8]

Ambrose (340-397)

He was made bishop of Milan before he was baptized and was instrumental in the conversion of Augustine. Ambrose, like the Judaizers, believed women to be ontologically inferior to men and, influenced by Gnosticism, relating them to the flesh and unbelief. He wrote: "Whoever does not believe is a woman. . . " but "the woman who believes is elevated to male completeness and to a measure of the stature of the fulness of Christ . . . she is free from her physical sex . . . the frivolity of youth and the talkativeness of old age."[9] Like the Greek Church Fathers, he reckoned a woman equal to a man after conversion.

Following the teaching of Epiphanius, he believed man to be superior to woman because of man's warm nature and intellectual capacity: "Thus woman is inferior to man, she is part of him, she is under his command. Sin began with her, she must wear this sign, the veil."[10]

Augustine (354-430)

Augustine was a clever, clear thinker and has been credited with laying the groundwork for a theology which lasted for a millennium. His *City of God* is still considered a classic and it strongly swayed the thinking of such Reformers as Calvin and Luther.

Before his conversion he was a Manichean, mixing Buddhism, Gnosticism, and the dualism of Zorastrianism. Manicheism demanded strict asceticism, celibacy and austere living since the Manichean lifestyle symbolized the struggle between light and darkness and the warfare between good and evil. However, his theology was more mental than moral. Tradition says he lived with a common-law wife for fifteen years until his mother forced him to abandon the woman because she wasn't in his social status. But that wasn't the end of his escapades. He began living with a mistress in what must have been a tortured relationship. He hated the carnal marriage connection but lived with her anyway.

After his conversion the Manichean influence continued coloring his reasoning. He decided women weren't created in God's image, only men were, contradicting 1 Corinthians 11:2-12 and Genesis 1:26, 27; both passages say God made them male and female in His image.

Even after his conversion, his former philosophy surfaced, especially the Gnostic idea of dualism, which labeled man the superior spirit while the woman was likened to the inferior flesh. "Flesh stands for the woman" he wrote, "and the spirit for the husband . . . because the latter rules, the former is ruled. Woman stands under the lordship of man and possesses no authority; she can neither teach, or be a witness." His emphatic opinion was without scriptural or historical proof except the oral law of the Jews, which made the same statement.

The truth is, women were witnesses; some were biblical prophets. They witnessed to Christ's resurrection, they exercised the same spiritual authority as any other believer, and some taught. Augustine's statements go against the grain of the history of the early apostolic church and his own Catholic Church since women were ordained as teaching deacons well into the late fourth century. As great and influential as Augustine proved himself to be, he was nevertheless a product of the thinking of the age in which he lived and studied. Unfortunately, his teaching on the role of women—as well as other doctrines—was wrong! His statement that women can't be witnesses was Talmudic, certainly not Scriptural.

These brief statements, taken from both Greek and Latin Fathers, clearly show the progressive decline of women's status and acceptance in the church after the middle second century. Judaism's influence is discernable in many areas of Christian tradition, especially the hierarchal structure of the church. The Fathers adapted the Jewish male-superior attitude and followed the same faulty reasoning based on untruths, superstitions and prejudices. Some of them were outspoken misogynists, most were celibates with a distaste for marriage and the normal sexual relationship (which God called good), and few were able to handle their biological relationships with women. By the fifth century the church's mistrust and misunderstanding of women was complete; the women were fully back in bondage again.

What Happened?

Both the Bible and history declare the acceptance of women as equals, both spiritually and socially, in the church during the apostolic age even though the new Christian Church was accepted as part of Judaism. Even during the Roman destruction of Jerusalem in A.D.70, many Jewish Christians fought alongside Israel.

The rabbis mistrusted but cautiously accepted them as one of the several religious parties existing within Judaism. Later in A.D. 132, Bar-Cochba proclaimed himself the Messiah and led Israel's final rebellion against their Roman masters. It lasted three years and resulted in the Roman victors denying the Jews entry to the city and the Temple. To this day Judaism has no sacrificial system or priesthood.

The Jews, for the most part, had accepted Bar-Cochba as their long-overdue Messiah, but the Christians rejected him, knowing Christ to be the true Messiah. Consequently, the embittered rabbis totally rejected the Christians for refusing to fight alongside them. The break between Christianity and Judaism was complete. The infant church was now on her own but the influence and security of Judaism's structured system was deeply ingrained.

The Development of a Professional Priesthood

According to the New Testament record the original church pattern was amazingly simple in both worship and governmental structure. Paul spoke of apostles, prophets, evangelists, pastors and teachers who were called elders, and deacons who were ministers (servants). The apostle said the sole purpose of these ministries (Eph. 4:8,11) was for the building up of the entire church, for equipping them for the work of service or ministry (Eph. 4:12, 13). "We are to grow up in all aspects into Him, who is the head, even Christ, from whom the whole body, being fitted and held together by that which every joint supplies, according to the proper working of each individual part, causes the growth of the body for the building up of itself in love" (Eph. 4:15-16). In 1 Corinthians 14:26 Paul left a crystal-clear picture of how the apostolic church functioned as as worshiping body: "When you assemble, each one has a psalm, has a teaching, has a revelation, has an interpretation . . ." The service was free flowing, simple, unstructured and not liturgical. Paul's main concern was that these functions be orderly and without confusion since everyone participated including the women (Gal. 3:28).

I can't find any scriptural evidence that this original church, established and blessed by Christ, copied either religious or political patterns. Actually, the Lord cautioned His disciples about their desire to exercise power and authority. They wanted to know who was the greatest, who was in charge, and who would be chosen above the others. Jesus answered, "You know that those who are are recognized as rulers of the Gentiles lord it over them; and their great men exercise authority over them. But it is not so among you, but whoever wishes to become great among you shall be your servant; and whoever wishes to be first among you shall be slave of all" (Mark 10:42-43).

He forbade His apostles and followers to copy the clothing and attitudes of the Pharisees who wore special clothing that set them apart as religious. They demanded special seats in the synagogues, salutations in the marketplaces, and special titles. "But you are not to be called rabbi, for you have one teacher, and you are all brethren. And call no man your father on earth for you have one Father, who is in heaven" (Matt. 23:8-9 RSV). Obviously, Jesus wasn't referring to one's natural biological father, since He used such a term when He taught His disciples how to pray. "Our Father" is from an Aramaic word, *Abba,* meaning "daddy." What Jesus said was not to call anyone on earth your "spiritual father" since we have only one such Father, God alone!

The title "priest" or "reverend" is foreign to the New Covenant Scriptures. Jesus never called himself a priest nor did He call, or authorize His disciples to call themselves priests. Christ's priesthood is described in Hebrews 3:1 as the "High Priest of our confession," and in Hebrews 5:5-6 as a perpetual priesthood likened to the priesthood of Melchizedek. Both Christ and Melchizedek had neither beginning or ending of days; therefore neither had any successors. If Christ has a perpetual priesthood then He has no substitutes. "But He, on the other hand, because He abides forever, holds His priesthood permanently" (Heb. 7:24). His sacrifice was complete and final! "Nor was it that He should offer Himself often, as the high priest enters the holy place year by year with blood not his own" (Heb. 9:25-26). "For by one offering He has perfected for all time these who are sanctified" (Heb. 10:14).

Rather than laying the groundwork for an exclusive, professional, all-male ministry, Christ carefully guarded against such a hierarchy. The Church is called a "royal priesthood" offering "spiritual sacrifices" through Christ the High Priest. The Master said the believer is part of a Kingdom of priests (Rev. 1:6).

Paul made it clear that Christ's high priesthood began when He was raised from the dead. Hebrews 5 says Christ did not glorify himself so as to *become* (meaning He was not so before a certain time) a high priest, but He who said to Him: "Thou art My Son, Today I have begotten Thee" (Heb. 5:5) followed by "Thou art a priest forever According to the order of Melchizedek" (Heb. 7:17). The key to the time of this high priestly ministry is "Today I have begotten thee," a quote from Psalm 2:7. However, Paul, speaking by divine inspiration, said this "begetting" took place at the resurrection. Acts 13:30 sets the context: "God raised Him from the dead." Then verse 22: "God has fulfilled this promise to our children in that He raised up Jesus, as it is also written in the second Psalm, 'Thou art My Son; today I have begotten Thee.' " Christ Jesus provided the perfect ransom price, and offered it for all sins of all time, perfecting those who are sanctified, making it impossible and unnecessary that His sacrifice be repeated. Therefore, the office of a professional priesthood is scripturally unnecessary.

However, as the church organized beyond the New Testament pattern, necessitated by growth (so say the apologists), it soon lost sight of its true purpose and mystery (Eph. 3:8-10). The apostolic worship was one of exuberant praise (Eph. 5:18-20), spiritual sacrifices (Heb. 13:15), individual participation (1 Cor. 14:26) with each believer adding to the edification of the whole body (1 Cor. 12:7; Eph. 4:12-16). As the free-flowing, Spirit-led meeting crystallized into a more formal and finally a purely ritualistic service, there wasn't any place for biblical praise or individual gift ministries. Everything became centered in one person, the priest. One of the most powerful results of the Charismatic Renewal is the restoration of biblical praise and worship and the corresponding gifts of the Spirit and personal ministries, and . . . the manifest presence of the Lord (Acts 15:15-17).

Because it is always easier to look backward, we can say how unfortunate it was that the concept of every believer being a "priest" or "minister" evolved into a sacerdotal priesthood "signed with a special character to act in the person of Christ, in His very image."[11] The church then had a specially chosen ministry which alone had Christ's authority to stand between the people and God. Without a doubt, that is why the spiritual gifts ceased around the second century. The Holy Spirit was systematically shut out of the services and His people excluded from all ministry.

By the time of Augustine, the ordination of priests was a sacrament and the ministry the exclusive right of the sacerdotal priesthood. The ministries of both lay men and women disappeared. Women were no longer ordained as deacons "due to their inferiority." Clement of Rome said bishops were those who have blamelessly and in holiness offered up sacrifices."[12]

With women there was also the question of their uncleanness. The Old Testament was explicit when dealing with any form of uncleanness approaching the Temple. Anyone with a seminal discharge, menstruation or running sores was considered unclean (Lev. 12:1-8; 15:16-24). Because there wasn't any provision for women priests in Israel, it seemed natural to exclude women from the church priesthood. The Church Fathers assumed God was male and bearded; therefore, all His representatives should be male in keeping with the visible sign of man's masculinity, the beard. Once the office of the priest was viewed in this light there were strong arguments for excluding women from the priesthood.[13]

The fallacy of this reasoning is evident: God is neither male nor female. Christ was male, to be sure, but God is Spirit (John 4:24) and sexless—sex is a biological necessity for reproduction. Man's beard is the result of hormones; women with excessive testosterone also grow beards. The idea that God is bearded is Jewish and we've dealt with this already. It is neither factual, scientific, nor scriptural. If this reasoning were correct and we carried it to a logical application, then the visible representative of the church would be a woman since the church is called the "bride of Christ" (2 Cor. 11:2; Rev. 21:2).

Edward Echlin, Catholic priest, wrote a paper, *The Deacon in the Church, Past and Future,"*[14] outlining the gradual decline of the diaconate. During the third century, around the time of the Council of Nicea, sacerdotalism replaced the simple believer's meeting. By the fourth century, the ecclesiastical structure was entrenched with a male-only priesthood legislated by church hierarchy. Echlin's purpose was to trace the decline of the deacon's role, but his awareness of the growth of the sacramental church corresponds with the decline of both lay men's and women's ministries. During the Council of Trent in 1563, called to counteract the Reformation that was shaking Europe, an unsuccessful attempt was made to restore the diaconate, but it wasn't until Vatican II that a permanent diaconate was restored to the Roman Church after an absence of more than a thousand years.

Pope Paul VI said on February 20, 1971, "Is the existence of a priesthood really justified in the economy of the New Testament?" He recognized the end of the Levitical priesthood and the sole mediatorship of Christ. He said that every believer belongs to the royal priesthood established by Christ and that true worship isn't ritual but in "spirit and truth."[15] In 1965 he approved a statement concerning women which ruled that the

Catholic Church is opposed to *all* forms of discrimination based on sex. "For in truth, it must still be regretted that fundamental personal rights are not yet being universally honored. Such is the case of a woman who is denied the right and freedom to choose a husband, to embrace a state of life, or to acquire an education or cultural benefits equal to those recognized for men."[16]

Hans Kung, a controversial, outspoken Catholic theologian, questioned the concept of a professional priesthood endowed with special privileges and authority. The priesthood of all believers extends to every area of Christian worship since every believer has direct access to God without mediators, he said, agreeing with Pope Paul VI. Each believer can freely offer to God prayers, praise, thanksgiving and supplications. He noted Christ's command to preach the gospel to all the world was not given just to the Twelve, but to the entire church. The commands concerning baptism, the Eucharist, and binding and loosing (absolution) were given to all His disciples, and not just the Twelve.[17]

This short survey of the development of an all-male ministry excluding women is given to show the drift away from binding apostolic patterns. As the church slipped into an acknowledged apostasy, the ministry of the Holy Spirit ceased. I was forced to uncover this trail of progressing disobedience within the Catholic Church since it was the prevailing Institution for more than 1200 years until the Reformation. Since the Reformation, many Protestant communions have adopted the same unscriptural thinking regarding the ministry of women.

On December 7, 1965, Pope Paul VI said, "However, it is the church's tradition that women are to be excluded from the priesthood, and this tradition is adhered to at the present time." The Declaration, *Gaudium et Spes,* recognized that patristic authors (the ante-Nicene fathers) strongly influenced the policy of excluding women from the leadership in the

Roman Catholic Church. It acknowledged that these writers are not beyond reproach. In the writings of the Fathers, "one will find the undeniable influence of prejudices unfavourable to women," and medieval scholastic doctors "often present arguments . . . that modern thought would have difficulty in admitting or would even rightly reject." However, the statement affirms that, "Since that period and up to our own time . . . the practice has enjoyed peaceful and universal acceptance."[18]

It is admitted then, that the rejection of women from the ministry doesn't rest upon revealed Scripture, but upon the opinions of patristic church leaders with personal anti-women prejudices and hatreds. It rests upon faulty information and the ignorance of medieval scholars whose conclusions Pope Paul VI said can't be accepted. He admitted "sacred tradition" is wrong. However, it will be continued since it has been practiced peacefully for so many years.

However, the Church of the risen Christ doesn't operate on tradition, faulty exegesis or personal prejudices but upon truth! Jesus said that whatsoever was not of faith was sin! The practice of eliminating deacons and laymen's ministries, and excluding women from all ministry, is admittedly wrong. It's now time to repent!

Chapter Eighteen Notes

1. Leonard Swidler, *Biblical Affirmations of Women* (Philadelphia, PA: Westminister Press, 1979), p. 342.
2. *Fathers of the Church,* tr. R. Arbesmann, E. Daily & E. Qualin (New York: Fathers of the Church, 1959).
3. George Tavard, *Women in Christian Tradition* (South Bend, IN: University of Notre Dame Press, 1973), p. 68.
4. *Patrologia Graeca* (New York: Adlers Foreign Books), Vol. 10, Col. 1282.
5. Ibid., Vol. 42, Col. 740.
6. Leonard Swidler, op. cit., p. 343.
7. Katherine Bushnell, *God's Word to Women* (1923; privately reprinted by Ray Munson, North Collins, NY), p. 362.
8. Leonard Swidler, op. cit., p. 346.
9. *Patrologia Latina* (New York: Adlers Foreign Books), Vol. 15, Col. 1844.
10. Ibid., Vol. 17, Col. 253.
11. Margaret Howe, *Women and Church Leadership* (Grand Rapids, MI: Zondervan, 1982), p. 100, quoting "The Order of Priesthood," *Our Sunday Visitor* 1978.
12. *Fathers of the Church,* 1:44, Letter to the Corinthians 44:4.
13. W. Phipps, "The Sex of God," *Journal of Ecumenical Studies* 1979, Vol. 6, No 1, pp. 515-517.
14. New York: Alba House, 1971.
15. *The Teachings of Pope Paul VI* (Washington, DC: U.S. Catholic Conference Publications Office, 1972) pp. 223-310.
16. "The Church Today," *Documents of Vatican II,* ed. W.M. Abbott (New York: Corpus, 1966), pp. 227-228.

17. Margaret Howe, op. cit., p. 97, quoting Hans Kung, *The Church,* trans. Ray and Rosaleen Ockenden (New York: Sheed and Ward, 1967), pp. 363-387.
18. Margaret Howe, op. cit., p. 132.

19

Jesus' Attitude Toward Women

All four gospels openly express Jesus' attitude toward women. It was never negative. He uplifted their social status by publicly associating with them. He used them as illustrations expressing eternal truths. He never rebuked them for violating religious taboos or overstepping traditions. Women followed Him as His disciples, some apparently having left prominent families behind. He refused to honor, follow, vindicate or accept many of the traditional laws which kept women in bondage. And all this within a framework which said, "Woman is in all things inferior to the man" and "Rather should the words of the Torah be burned than entrusted to a woman."

The explanation that woman's social standing had changed by the time Jesus ministered, so His attitudes weren't that radical, is invalid. The available sources, such as Josephus, Philo, the Dead Sea Scrolls and the oral law itself all underscore the prevalent idea that woman was inferior to man. Rather than the trend being uplifting for women, the evidence indicates that just prior to and after the beginning of the Common Era their status worsened. Nor is there any reason to believe that the Lord's male disciples had different attitudes, since they were practicing Jews; yet they faithfully and honestly recorded the Lord's words and actions toward women without prejudice or comment.

I've left this vital aspect of our study for the last chapter since Jesus ministered between the two covenants. He closed out the old by fulfilling all its demands and ushered in the new. As the Mediator of the New Covenant His Word is all-important! As God's only begotten Son and the express image of the Father (Heb. 1:3), He knew the true intent behind each piece of legislation given to Moses. Yet during His ministry He seemingly contradicted, changed or worked against the commonly accepted rabbinical interpretations of the Mosaic law.

For example: Jesus often said, "It has been said" referring to Moses, the law or the prophets, but then He added, "But I say unto you" and then modified what had been said. When the Pharisees questioned Him about whether a man could divorce his wife for any reason He said, "What therefore God has joined together, let no man separate" (Matt. 19:6).

Back came their rebuttal. "Why then did Moses command to give her a certificate and divorce her?" They alluded to Deuteronomy 24:1-4 and they were correct in what that part of the Torah, the law, said. It was God's law; however, Jesus gave them the reason behind this piece of stopgap legislation.

"Because of your hardness of heart . . . but from the beginning it has not been this way." Moses allowed divorce because they were insensitive, hard-hearted and sinful. Another time Jesus said, "It was said, 'You shall not commit adultery; but I say to you, that every one who looks on a woman to lust for her has committed adultery with her already in his heart" (Matt. 5:27-28). Notice the contrast!

The Mosaic law only dealt with the commission of sin. Until a person was actually murdered, the law wasn't broken. Hatred, jealousy and those things which precipitate the act of murder weren't considered. They couldn't be since man hadn't been born again. But under the New Covenant the attitude changed. Our Lord went much deeper and touched the root cause for these actions which can mature into full-blown acts of sin. This principle is important in understanding His attitude toward women since He frequently rebutted the rabbinical interpretations of the Mosaic law. The "It has been said," whether the Mosaic legislation, the rabbinical interpretations of that law, or the social mores and customs of the day, must give way to His "But I say unto you" as the Word Christians obey.

Before we examine our Lord's attitude toward women we must consider the argument that Jesus ministered under the law, that His instructions were for the Jews, and that since they refused His offer of the Kingdom it was postponed until the millennium. This novel interpretation has absolutely no scriptural basis. It is a human interpretation that dates back no earlier than the late nineteenth century. Christ came to destroy the works of Satan, to bring in righteousness and establish the reign of God (1 John 3:8; Col. 1:13; Rom. 14:17). He did!

Jesus Recognized Woman's Personal Worth

Luke 10:38-42 records a visit Jesus made to the home of Martha and Mary, an event that portrayed His personal attitude toward the prevailing Jewish practices. Mary sat at His feet listening to His Word, taking the posture of a male student (v. 39). When Luke said, "Mary, who moreover was listening to the Lord's word," he affirmed her discipleship.

Meanwhile, Martha, her sister, labored in the customary role for women: she served. She accepted the female's place while Mary assumed the male's position. Both Jesus and Mary knew that the oral law kept women from studying the Torah. The proper place for the woman was in the house serving her husband and sons. When Martha saw Mary's bold action she exhorted Jesus to "tell her to help me."

Here was the Lord's opportunity to set the record straight for Christian women for all time and correct Mary's brazen boldness, but He didn't. Instead, He let her remain seated at His feet and refused to tell her to help Martha. He didn't remind her the proper role for women was serving the men. Rather, He accepted her as an individual person fully capable of making her own choices. "Martha," the Lord said, "You are worried and bothered about so many things; but only a few things are necessary, really only one: for Mary has chosen the good part, which shall not be taken away from her" (vv. 41, 42).

With these words He stripped away centuries of male domination and religious tradition. Basically, He was saying, "It has been said" women belong in the home, "but I say to you the most important thing is knowing the Word. Mary has chosen the best thing!" As far as the Son of God was concerned, the Talmudic traditions, the patriarchal positions, and woman's social stigma were voided once and for all. Mary's choice to study the Word was more important than tradition. He recognized her personal worth, her intelligence and her rational choices to be as valid as a man's. He refused to recognize Jewish traditions as Lord of the New Covenant!

An interesting observation about Mary comes to light in John's gospel. She alone, of all the Lord's disciples and intimate friends, grasped the real purpose for his messiahship. None of His disciples, including the Twelve, really knew Him. Peter opposed Him when He spoke of his impending death. The disciples abandoned Him during His greatest ordeal, the cross. On the day he ascended back to heaven they were still looking for a military-political Messiah who would crush Rome and restore Israel's national glory (Acts 1:6). When Jesus talked to Martha before raising her dead brother, she refused to believe what He said about himself: "I am the resurrection and the life!"

What about Mary's knowledge of her Lord? In John 12:1-7 is another account of a supper, again at the home of Martha and Mary and Lazarus, the brother Jesus had raised from the dead. As usual, "Martha served" (v. 2), but Mary not only remained in the same room where men were eating (a no-no according to rabbinical law), she took a bottle of expensive perfume, broke it and poured it over the Master's feet. Then she loosed her hair and, letting it fall naturally to its full length, she wiped His feet. Jesus accepted her devotion and said nothing.

When a Jewish woman let her hair hang naturally she was uncovered. If she did it publicly it was grounds for mandatory divorce. Such was the rabbinical law and its strict demands. Again Jesus told those who objected to "let her alone, in order that she may keep it for the day of My burial" (v. 7). Only Mary understood the purpose of His necessary death and honored Him. Meanwhile, Jesus defended her actions, honored her by having it recorded in the Scriptures, and set aside more rabbinical customs. This incident is enlightening since only Mary is recorded as sitting at His feet. It's possible the other disciples sat there also, but there's evidence they really didn't hear what He said.

There were other occasions when Jesus defended a woman's personal worth as an intelligent, thinking person with feelings. In Luke 11:27-28 a woman cried from the crowd, "Blessed is the womb that bore You, and the breasts at which you nursed." What else could a traditional woman say under the circumstances? According to Jewish law the woman was created for man's pleasure, to be his possession and bear his children. She was saved by bearing him male children. That's why she cried as she did. However, Jesus put an end to this kind of baby-machine mentality. On the contrary, "blessed are those who hear the word of God, and observe it."

Isn't it significant that this woman's statement is preserved in the Bible? The Bible is filled with marvelous miracles, major events and so many important activities, but John said maybe the world couldn't hold the books if everything Jesus said and did were recorded. Why was this event recorded? The content stresses the importance of God's Word above that of a person's gender, again opening the way for women to freely partake as learners and disciples of the Word.

Jesus, Women and Marriage

Thousands of words of instruction were spoken and written by the rabbis concerning women, their place in the home and their obedience to men. Doubtless Jesus' revolutionary attitude toward marriage made Him extremely unpopular. For example: the oral law permitted a man to divorce his wife, or wives, for any reason, at his discretion, but a woman couldn't divorce her husband under any circumstances. A man could have as many wives as he desired but a woman would never have more than one husband. A man chose his wife but a woman had no choice in who her husband would be. These were the customs Jesus resisted.

In Matthew 19:3-10 the Pharisees asked Jesus about the lawfulness of a man divorcing his wife for any cause. The Pharisees were arguing over the contradictory rabbinical teachings. One said a man can't divorce his wife except for immorality, while another said he could divorce her for any reason. Which rabbi was right, since both opinions were part of the oral law? Gently, but firmly, the Lord cleared away the haziness. He told them that in the beginning God made them male and female and joined them together as one. Therefore, let no man separate what God has joined.

222

Then they asked why Moses permitted divorce. "Because of the hardness of your hearts," Jesus said.

Why did Moses permit divorce? Because of hardness, or insensitive, uncaring, calloused, nonfeeling attitudes. Who divorced, the man or the woman? Only the man; therefore, because of the man's insensitive, uncaring attitude, God allowed divorce to protect the woman. Since it wasn't God's plan from the beginning, it was the result of sin. In other words, Moses permitted divorce because of sin!

He continued, "And I say to you, whoever divorces his wife, except for immorality, and marries another commits adultery" (v. 9). The disciples stumbled at this and concluded: "It is better not to marry." In other words, if a man can't throw his wife away at will, why get married?

When Jesus restricted a man to one wife he abolished polygamy, still practiced in first century C.E. Mark included a devastating statement Matthew left out: ". . . and if she herself divorces her husband . . ." (Mark 10:12). Jewish women couldn't divorce their husbands since they were the men's possessions. Not only did Jesus end easy divorce, He put an immediate end to polygamy and gave the women permission to put their husbands away if guilty of immorality.

In Matthew 22:23-30 the liberal Sadducees challenged Jesus with a question, "If a man dies, having no children, his brother as next of kin shall marry his wife, and raise up an offspring to his brother [they quoted Moses in Deut. 25:5]. Now there were seven brothers with us, and the first married and died, and having no offspring left his wife to his brother; so also the second, and the third, down to the seventh. And last of all, the woman died. In the resurrection therefore whose wife of the seven shall she be? For they all had her." Jesus knew it was a trick question since the Sadduccees didn't believe in the resurrection. Nevertheless, He used the question to defend the rights of the woman as an individual.

"For in the resurrection they neither marry, nor are given in marriage, but are like the angels in heaven" (v. 30). In other words, a woman isn't anyone's possession to be passed along like a family heirloom. She is a unique person in herself, and not man's property to be disposed of as he desires.

When the woman taken in the act of adultery was brought to Jesus for judgment He attacked the obvious male hypocrisy (John 8:1-11). Both the scribes and Pharisees knew that Moses' law demanded the death of both the man and woman guilty of adultery, but where was the man caught in the very act with her? He was excused while the woman was paraded before Jesus and publicly blamed. Rather than agreeing with the religionists, Jesus wrote on the ground, and whatever He wrote caused them to walk away defeated. I wouldn't be surprised if what He wrote was Leviticus 20:10 where God said both the adulterer and adulteress shall be put to death.

Jesus Healed All Kinds of Women

As Israel's messiah and mankind's deliverer he came to set the captives free (Luke 4:18). In so doing He violated many Jewish traditions and laws. The rabbis resisted laying their hands on women whether they were clean or unclean, socially acceptable or public prostitutes, but Jesus did many times.

Mark 5:24-34 records the scene where a woman with an issue of blood was marvelously healed when she touched Jesus' garment. She didn't ask Him to touch her, knowing the rabbinical law said she was unclean and untouchable as long as she had any form of bodily discharge, and anyone touching her would be unclean. Her bold decision was made out of desperation.

For more than twelve years, she had been kept out of the temple. For more than twelve years the priests and rabbis ostracized her as displeasing to God. According to Leviticus 15:19-30, which had been brutally tortured and twisted beyond sensibility, the interpreters said the victim was unclean as well as anyone who touched her.

When she touched Jesus, He instantly knew someone had touched Him with faith. He felt virtue leave His body. When He looked down and saw this pitiful woman, He didn't rebuke her for making Him unclean. He commended her before the crowd. Her sickness had not rendered Him unclean nor had she broken God's law. In so doing He nullified the rabbinical law that menstruation was a curse from God because Eve sinned.

He healed a woman on the Sabbath, another no-no (Luke 13:10-17). When He saw her crippled condition He said, "It isn't right that this daughter of Abraham be bound by the devil," and He loosed her. His term "daughter of Abraham" was theologically unacceptable to the Jews since they believed that only the circumcised male Jew was a son of the covenant. Man's exclusive domain was gradually caving in.

And there was a gentile woman, a Syrophoenician, whose daughter was demonized. When she asked the apostles to help her they pushed her aside. She persisted until they finally asked the Lord to stop her. Undaunted, she pestered Jesus until He told her to go home, that her daughter was healed, the first gentile child to receive healing under His ministry. A woman, a non-Jew, bold and brassy, received healing when it was supposed to be the exclusive right of the Jews. God's love and mercy transcends man's futile religious beliefs.

Jesus and the Prostitutes

To the pious Jew, the only person lower than a tax collector or swineherd was a public prostitute. Whether by intent or casual circumstance, Jesus told the chief priests and scribes that the politicians and prostitites would enter the Kingdom of God ahead of them. It isn't any wonder these leaders worked continually until they finally found an excuse to kill Him.

While dining with Simon the Pharisee, an immoral woman entered the same room where the men were eating. Kneeling at the Lord's feet she poured a flask of expensive ointment on them, kissed them, and, like Mary, uncovered her head by loosing her hair and wiped Jesus' feet. It was a touching scene but one that scandalized Simon, the law keeper. He knew the law forbade women speaking in public, let alone immoral women. He watched as Jesus let her kiss His feet, touch Him, a rabbi, and uncover her head, removing the sign that she was an inferior creature under male subjugation. Jesus responded by forgiving her sins and refusing to correct her totally unacceptable conduct. He commended her for her devotion, love, humility and faith (Luke 7:36-50).

Jesus and the Samaritan Woman

Religious nationalism was alive and well during our Lord's earthly ministry. Long after Christ's resurrection and ascension back to heaven, long after the Pentecostal outpouring, Peter still objected to associating with a gentile (Acts 10:28). "You yourselves know how unlawful it is for a man who is a Jew to associate with a foreigner or to visit him . . ." After Peter returned to Jerusalem (Cornelius had not only been born again but Jesus baptized him in the Holy Spirit), the apostles and the circumcised took issue with him. "You went to uncircumcised men and ate with them" (11:3).

In John 4:7-30 there is a powerful scene in which Jesus approaches a Samaritan woman and asks her for a drink of water. The woman's reaction is instant and curt: "How is it that You, being a Jew, ask me for a drink since I am a Samaritan woman?" Oh, the mercy and love of God that even a Samaritan woman, considered a nothing by the pious Jewish male, could talk with the Lord of Glory and be treated with respect and dignity! Jesus offered her a drink of eternal water that would give her eternal life. Once again Jesus flouted traditions that were designed to keep women in bondage.

Jesus and the Widows of Israel

The scribes, lawyers who interpreted the law, had a reputation for fleecing and robbing widows by taking what little they possessed. In Mark 12:38-40 Jesus sternly rebuked those scribes who devoured widows' houses. Without husbands they were twice non-persons, without income, husbands or standing before the law. Yet it was a widow and prophetess who met Jesus when His parents presented Him at the Temple for circumcision, and she prophesied over Him (Luke 2:36-38).

Jesus used the sacrificial giving of a widow's mite to illustrate the true principle of giving (Luke 21:1-4). He used a widow with a weak social standing to show the power of persevering prayer as she overcame the reluctance of a judge to restore her property (Luke 18:1-8). Jesus raised the dead son of the widow of Nain knowing she had no one to provide for her. Moved with pity, He said, "Do not weep!" and gave her back her only son (Luke 7:11-17). Realizing the shabby way widows were treated, He made sure His mother was properly cared for after His death. Looking down from the cross He told John, "Behold, your mother!" and to Mary, "Woman, behold, your son!"

Jesus said the Jews nullified the Word of God with their traditions. Knowing the rabbinical laws weren't inspired by God He didn't hesitate to overrule them. Later, the Holy Spirit inspired James to write that caring for the orphans and the widows in their affliction is pure religion and acceptable to God (James 1:27).

Jesus Had Women Disciples

Never before nor since have women enjoyed the acceptance as full persons they did under Christ's earthly ministry. He numbered women among His disciples.

The word disciple comes from a Greek word meaning "learner," one who followed the teacher closely, living and learning at His feet. It's interesting to note that the word used for the women who "served" Jesus is *diakoneo,* the basic word for "deacon," and it aptly describes the ministry of the women Jesus counted as His disciples (Mark 15:40-41; Matt. 27:55-56). Some of these women were from prominent families with wealthy backgrounds. Some left home to follow Him, as apparently did Joanna (the wife of Chuza, Herod's chief steward), and traveled openly with Him. Again, Jesus overturned the cultural and religious taboos of the day.

In a way, Jesus dismantled the patriarchal family system that kept women in servitude. It was a repressive system and it is still practiced in Africa and the Middle East. By allowing these women to be His disciples He accepted them on equal footing with the men He chose. Even though Jesus told the rich young ruler about leaving house, wife, brothers, sisters, parents or children for His sake and the Kingdom of God (Luke 18:29), He was not against the family unit. He was against the repressive use of women as servants and property of the patriarchal lord of the family. Any system, then or now, that prevents anyone from serving God and growing in knowledge of the Word is wrong (see Matt. 10:28-30; 34-38; 19:29; Luke 18:28-30).

Jesus and the Women at the Cross

During the worst ordeal of His life, "all the disciples left Him and fled" (Matt. 26:56), that is, all except the women. John the beloved was at the foot of the cross with Jesus' mother (John 19:25-27) but the rest of the disciples fled in terror for fear of the Jews. The Lord defended the women during His ministry, and they now stood beside Him during the terror of the cross.

It was the women who prepared the bruised, broken body for burial, and they were present when Joseph of Arimathea placed the dead body in his personal tomb. They were there when the Roman authorities sealed the tomb. The women were the first ones to return to the grave after the Sabbath to finish anointing the body (Mark 15:43-47; Matt. 27:57-61; Luke 23:50-56). And these women were the first ones to witness the angelic visitation and the Lord's resurrection (Mark 16:1-6). Meanwhile, His male disciples were still in hiding.

When Jesus chose evangelists to take the message of His resurrection to His hiding disciples, He chose the women (Matt. 28:1-8). These women were doubly commissioned. First, the angel told them to go tell the disciples, and to tell Peter, since he was the first to deny the Lord, that Jesus was risen and would meet them in Galilee (Mark 16:7). Then the Lord himself met them and greeted them, telling them to take the word of His resurrection to His brethren (Matt. 28:9, 10).

Luke gave us the reaction of the apostles when the women told them the good news. "And these words appeared to them as nonsense, and they would not believe them" (24:11). However, Peter ran to the tomb and saw the empty linen wrappings.

Jesus Appeared to Women First

Three of the four gospels say that Jesus appeared to Mary Magdalene first and later to His disciples. As a teacher, Jesus knew that the law said women couldn't be witnesses since they were unreliable. Yet He purposely chose women first to carry the good news of the most important event in history, His resurrection. And the apostles were the first unbelievers until He appeared to them on that first day of the week. Jesus sent the women *(apostelein)* to bear witness to the apostles *(apostolous,* Luke 24:10). Actually, Mary was an apostle to the apostles and was so called by some Church Fathers. At any rate He included women among those He personally chose to propagate the gospel of His Kingdom.

Interestingly, these women fulfilled the necessary qualifications for apostleship. When the eleven chose Judas' successor, Peter listed the requirements. "It is therefore necessary that of the men who have accompanied us all the time that the Lord Jesus went in and out among us—beginning with the baptism of John, until the day that He was taken up from us—one of these should become a witness with us of His resurrection" (Acts 1:21-22). Paul defended his right to be called an apostle by saying he had seen the risen Lord and personally talked with Him. With the exception of Peter's word "men," the women were fully qualified to bear witness as apostles, sent by the Lord. Earlier in this study we brought out the fact that the Jews would never accept the witness of any woman about any important matter. Therefore, a man was chosen as the successor of Judas since the twelve would witness primarily to the Jews. Still, Jesus chose to send the women to His apostles.

What can we say about Jesus' attitude toward women? It was positive, liberating and accepting. He defended them when they transgressed Jewish law if it was based on uninspired rabbinical interpretations. He didn't hesitate to withstand the social traditions and prejudices in order to free them. He accepted women as capable and fully equal with men in all things.

He closed the door to the Old Covenant and ushered in a New Covenant wherein there is neither Jew nor Greek, male nor female, only oneness in Christ. He set the captives free, both men and women, from all the bondages of sin, the curse, and religion.

Did Jesus say women can't teach? Does the Bible? Who did?

The Judaizers relying on the oral law of the Jews.

Should women remain bound because of Christian traditions that are only human interpretations? No more than the women serving under Christ's ministry remained bound to the Jewish traditions.

In this study I've sought answers for the unanswered questions that are raised whenever women in active ministry are discussed, and I've shared those findings with you. My conclusion is this: nowhere does the Bible from Genesis to maps forbid any woman from serving God in any capacity He calls and prepares her to fulfill.

Bibliography

Adams, Q., *Neither Male Nor Female,* (Dallas: Christ for the Nations, 1977).

Aid to Bible Understanding (New York: Watch Tower Tract and Bible Society, 1971).

The Ante-Nicene Fathers (Grand Rapids, MI: Eerdmans, 1979).

Bauer, Arndt, and Ginrich, *A Greek-English Lexicon of the New Testament* (Chicago: University of Chicago Press, 1958).

Beard, Helen, *Women in Ministry Today* (South Plainfield, NJ: Bridge Publishing, 1980).

Berry, George, *The Classic Greek New Testament* (New York: Folette Publishing, 1956).

Bushnell, Katherine, *God's Word to Women* (1923; privately reprinted by Ray Munson, North Collins, NY).

Buswell, James, *A Systematic Theology of the Christian Religion* (Grand Rapids, MI: Zondervan).

Calvin, John, *Commentaries* (Grand Rapids, MI: Associated Publishers and Authors).

Christenson, Larry, *The Christian Family* (Minneapolis: Bethany Fellowship, 1974).

Cohen, Abraham, *Everyman's Talmud* (New York: E.P. Dutton, 1949).

Davis, John, *Dictionary of the Bible* (Grand Rapids, MI: Baker Book House, 1981).

The Fathers of the Church, translated by Arbesmann, Daly and Qualin (New York: Fathers of the Church, 1959).

Foh, Susan, *Women and the Word of God* (Phillipsburg, NJ: Presbyterian and Reformed Publishing, Co., 1979).

Hagin, Kenneth, *The Woman Question* (Tulsa, OK: Kenneth Hagin Ministries, 1975).

Hicks, B., *And God Made Woman* (Jeffersonville, IN: Christ Gospel Churches, 1973).

Hodge, Charles, *Systematic Theology* (Grand Rapids, MI: Eerdmans, 1968).

Howe, Margaret, *Women and Church Leadership* (Grand Rapids, MI: Zondervan, 1982).

Kell, C.F., and Delitzsch, F., *Commentary on the Old Testament in Ten Volumes* (Grand Rapids, MI: Baker Book House, 1977).

Knight, George W. III, *The New Testament Teaching on the Role Relationship of Men and Women* (Grand Rapids, MI: Baker Book House, 1979).

Lesser, Isaac, *The Holy Bible* (Brooklyn, NY: Hebrew Publishing).

MacArthur, John, *Family Feuding and How to End It* (Panorama City, CA: Word of Grace Communications, 1981).

Matthew Henry's Commentary (Marshallton, DE: National Foundation for Christian Education).

Mead, Margaret, *Sex and Temperament in Three Primitive Societies* (New York: William Morrow and Co., 1973).

Miller, Madeliene S., and Lane, J., *Harper's Bible Dictionary* (New York: Harper and Row, 1952).

Moulton and Milligan, *Vocabulary of the Greek New Testament* (Grand Rapids, MI: Eerdmans, 1930).

Nicoll, W., *The Expositor's Greek New Testament* (Grand Rapids, MI: Eerdmans, 1967).

Palmer, F.H., *New Bible Dictionary* (London: JLVF, 1962).

Patrologia Graeca and *Patrologia Latina* (New York: Adlers Foreign Books; reprinted from the 1857 edition).

Penn-Lewis, Jessis, *Magna Charta of Woman* (Minneapolis: Bethany Fellowship, 1975).

The Pulpit Commentary (Grand Rapids, MI: Eerdmans, 1950).

Ramsay, W.M., *The Church in the Roman Empire* (Grand Rapids, MI: Baker Book House).

Rothacker, John, *The Public Ministry of Women* (Columbus, OH: John Rothacker Ministries, 1980).

Rubens, Alfred, *A History of Jewish Costume* (New York: Funk & Wagnalls, 1967).

Scanzoni, Letha, and Hardesty, Nancy, *All We're Meant to Be* (Waco, TX: Word Books, 1974).

Schaff, Philip, *History of the Christian Church* (Grand Rapids, MI: Eerdmans, 1910).

The Septuagint (Grand Rapids, MI: Zondervan, 1970).

Swidler, Leonard, *Biblical Affirmations of Women* (Philadelphia: Westminister Press, 1979).

Swidler, Leonard, *Women in Judaism* (Metuchen, NJ: Scarecrow Press, 1976).

The Talmud, edited by I. Epstein (New York: Rebecca Bennett Publishing, 1959).

Tavard, George, *Women in Christian Tradition* (South Bend, IN: Universityof Notre Dame Press, 1973).

Thayer, Joseph, *Greek-English Lexicon of the New Testament* (Grand Rapids, MI: Zondervan, 1968).

Tyros Greek Lexicon (London: Brown and Greek, 1825).

Vine, W.E., *Expository Dictionary of New Testament Words* (Old Tappan, NJ: Fleming H. Revell, 1966).